A JOB TO DIE FOR

WHY SO MANY AMERICANS ARE KILLED, INJURED OR MADE ILL AT WORK AND WHAT TO DO ABOUT IT

Lisa Cullen

Common Courage Press   Monroe, ME

363.110973
C 967 i

**Library of Congress Cataloguing in Publications Data is
available from the publisher on request.**

ISBN 1-56751-216-x paper
ISBN 1-56751-217-8 cloth

Common Courage Press
P.O. Box 702
Monroe, Maine 04951
207-525-0900; fax: 207-525-3068
orders-info@commoncouragepress.com

www.commoncouragepress.com

First Printing

About the Author

Lisa Cullen has been an industrial hygienist for 15 years and holds certification by the American Board of Industrial Hygiene. She is a volunteer for The FIGHT Project and a contributing editor for Occupational Hazards Magazine. She has written for Industrial Safety and Hygiene News, the American Industrial Hygiene Association and the National Safety Council.

In memory of George Granados, who would have read this
and cared enough to be outraged.

Dedicated to Andrew E. Cullen,
who made this book possible.

Contents

CHAPTER 1

Preventable Losses

The Personal Toll

"The doctors don't think the infection will kill me," Sue reports matter-of-factly. After seven years of surgeries, pain and dealing with workers' compensation insurance, she has resigned herself to life after occupational injury.

Sue was an experienced nurse with ten years invested at the same long-term health care facility when she requested a lifting hoist for one of her patients. The patient had Multiple Sclerosis (MS), and her legs were growing weak as the disease advanced. Sue's employer denied the hoist request and a few weeks later the patient's legs crumpled as Sue moved her from her bed to a wheelchair. With her arms around Sue's neck, the patient was close enough to hear a "pop noise." She started crying as Sue said, "I'm okay. These things happen."

Sue wasn't okay; her neck broke. When the patient's legs buckled, her body weight suddenly hung on her interlocked fingers behind Sue's neck. Snap.

Managing to work for three more weeks, Sue finally accepted that she was badly injured. Several operations later, her neck was "wired together," and she suffered multiple draining infections at the wound site. After antibiotic treatments, the wire became infected with an antibiotic resistant bacteria. "At times, it was like pea soup coming out of my neck," she says.

Sue's injury has touched all aspects of her life. She walks stiffly—partly from the injury and partly from the pain—and can't really rotate her head. She has a constant headache, suffers recurring fevers and has permanent and severe nerve damage. She can't drive and finds even sitting in a car difficult; the distance she can travel limits family outings.

Sue calmly describes the financial loss, the constant physical pain, and how she has trouble simply watching her daughter play volleyball because she can't sit on the bleachers. "The bleachers shake too much, especially when the team scores and everyone jumps to their feet."

The nurse in Sue describes her ever-present headache as an "occipital migraine headache" and that the infection is caused by a bacteria called MRSA, which stands for Methicillin Resistant Staphylococcus Aureus. She explains, "MRSA infections basically rot the bones away as it moves through them. It is usually found with amputations." Since the MRSA is in her neck bones, the spinal nerves encased by those degrading bones are becoming pinched, causing pain and loss of function.

Sue's neurological tests show her severe nerve damage. She is losing control of her arms; tasks requiring manual dexterity are moving slowly beyond her reach. Fighting to remain active, Sue recently purchased voice-activated software for her computer because she realizes that as her bones decay, she could eventually become paralyzed from the neck down.

It is this image of herself in a wheelchair that finally gets to Sue; fear and grief creep into her voice. MRSA may not kill her but the Sue that once was is gone and the Sue that is yet to be will have her nerves crushed so badly that she will probably be wheelchair bound and pain ridden. One day, she will probably awake as the patient with a nurse helping her from bed to wheelchair.

Sue's family shares her burden. Her husband recently suffered a massive heart attack. Sue explains, "He had been putting in lots of overtime to make up the money I am not making." Her 13-year-old daughter wrote "Tears," a poem reflecting painful lessons learned from witnessing her mother's ordeal. It begins:

Once vibrant, full of life filled with high expectations, dreams of the future:

Shattered within a moment, no notice of what lie ahead.

Work, work, work. Love your job, give 100% plus more;

Yet to find when you become injured on the job, it is almost clear to say life once known, will forever change with a rapid sweep as a fleeting memory once galore.

As I sit back and ponder;

Of the once total person I knew, now devastated through piles of bureaucracy.

I have to wonder;

The things that were taught to me of history were pure hypocrisy.

A woman who was educated, talented, giving, trusting, filled with hopes and dreams;

Now lives each day as a challenge, to begin each day anew.

A woman who supported her family, friends and others;

Now faces life's simple challenges each morning awaiting the clue...

The National Toll

Every day, 165 Americans die from occupational diseases and 18 more die from a work related injury. On the same day, more than 36,400 non-fatal injuries and 3,200 illnesses will occur in America's workplaces.[1] Each year, this unknown workplace epidemic extends into nearby communities to claim the lives of 218 innocent bystanders and injure another 68,000.[2]

America's millions of occupational diseases, deaths and injuries cost an unfathomable 155.5-billion dollars, annually; five times the cost of AIDS, three times the cost for Alzheimer's disease and almost as much as cancer.[3] This already unimaginable number grows by another 13 billion when property damage, police and fire protection, and costs to innocent bystanders are added.[4] We all bear the financial burden with reduced job opportunities, lower salaries, earlier social security payments, and higher costs for health insurance, workers' compensation and disability. The costs are nothing, however, compared with the toll paid in pain and suffering. Each year more than 66,700 dead workers[5] leave irrevocably changed families, coworkers and friends.

Despite its enormous toll, the epidemic of uncontrolled illnesses and injuries raging through our nation's workplaces moves quietly, its devastation too dispersed to be recognized by the public or the media. Still, millions of workers injured or made ill each year and their families struggle in a wake of personal pain and loss of income.

A typical day in the American workplace includes 165 occupational disease deaths[6] plus the following fatalities:

- 3 workers die in highway vehicle accidents
- 2 to 3 workers are shot (at least 1 works in a retail establishment)
- 2 workers die from falling, usually off ladders, roofs or scaffolds
- 1 worker is killed in a vehicle incident off a roadway (such as an overturned farm tractor or forklift)
- 1 worker dies after being struck by a vehicle
- 1 worker dies in an air, water or rail crash
- 1 worker dies after being struck by a falling object, such as by a tree during tree cutting, a brick falling off a scaffold, or a car falling off a jack during repair
- 1 worker is electrocuted
- 1 worker is killed in either a fire or explosion, from drowning or from inhaling a toxic substance

- 1 worker commits suicide on the job or because of a job-related incident

- 1 worker is killed by being caught in a machine or caught under collapsing materials, such as in a trench cave-in or engulfment in a grain bin.[7]

Even uncommon fatalities add up in the course of a year. Annually, 30 workers die the maddening and avoidable death of heatstroke; another 30 are poisoned to death by the sneaky, odorless carbon monoxide gas; 10 die from exploding tires (usually when inflating them); 12 farmers are gored or trampled to death and 8 workers inspecting or cleaning machinery are burned to death by escaping steam.

Accidents versus Foreseeable Consequences

An accident can be defined as an unexpected and unintentional happening that results in damage to people or property. Although it is common to say, "Hey, accidents happen," they are more complicated than that. In hindsight, most can be seen building from several causes, each representing a missed opportunity to step in and prevent the forthcoming damage. In fact, the safety and health profession is so averse to the term accident that the word incident has been widely substituted.

In the workplace, few real accidents occur because the surroundings and operations are known; therefore, hazards can be identified. When harm from those hazards can be foreseen, accidents can be prevented.

Most workplaces are manageable environments—employers can ventilate chemicals; shield against physical danger like burns, falls or amputations; and provide protective equipment. Once buildings, equipment, processes and chemicals are safe to use, employers can establish safe work procedures. They can further under-gird their accident prevention efforts with training, enforcement, employee involvement, safety inspections and medical surveillance.

A common 'accident' scenario is like that described in a recent safety management book. Illustrating how a 'freak accident' could have been prevented, it explains that a worker jumped off a forklift without shutting it down. The machine slipped into reverse, killing a coworker and damaging equipment.

At first glance, this seems like a typical accident; no one expected the machine to slip into reverse or anticipated that a coworker would be behind the forklift and in front of a wall. After a second look, blame might seem to fall squarely on the worker that exited the forklift without shutting it down, but stopping here does nothing to prevent a similar tragedy or learn from the loss.

In hindsight, the book describes the many factors that contributed to the fatality, including: a defective shutoff switch; lack of training for the forklift operator; improper maintenance of the forklift; broken back-up alarm; inadequate work-site inspection; and an insufficient process to take defective equipment out of service.[8] Each piece of the puzzle represents an overlooked or dismissed hazard that, if addressed, could have prevented the fatality.

Accidents don't just happen; they build. Like the forklift example, most have multiple causes and influences that could be addressed to prevent an incident. Employers often don't realize how significantly they risk employee safety or recognize how much more they can do to reduce risk—how preventable accidents are.

Although tougher to recognize, even rare hazards can be predicted. In 1990, for example, the UAW lost a millwright when he walked the roof of a foundry to replace a steel cable. Returning to the shop, he crossed a deteriorated section and fell through to his death. He was unaware that heating and cooling weakened that spot of the roof and that fragments had already fallen.[9] Diligent facility maintenance and inspections could have prevented this accident and this man's death.

Most jobs have expected, known hazards. Working in and near excavations, for example, poses the obvious risks of death or injury from cave-in. Also well known in the excavation business is the fact that certain soil types and other factors—things like water in the hole and previous soil disruption—increase the chances for a cave-in. Based on these factors, the OSHA standard prescribes appropriate sloping and benching requirements. When trenches or excavations collapse because sandy soil was piled right up to the edge, there is little room to claim it was an accident. One of the most horrifying ways to die is to be buried to your shoulders by soil, unable to inhale because your chest can't expand.

Like excavating, heavy equipment work near power lines carries the risk of electrocution. Workers die every year when machines, ladders and scaffolds contact electrical wires. Simply barricading the danger zone or de-energizing the lines are two immediate, life-saving solutions.

Chemical illness and death from overexposure are equally preventable. All U.S. manufacturers are legally bound to provide health and safety information on the chemicals they sell. The best information and technology, however, are useless when disregarded. The critical issue is foresight but many preventative steps are overlooked.

Although willful disregard of employee welfare does occur, most employers are not intentionally trying to maim or kill the very people that allow their businesses to operate. If Sue's employer, for example, was directly given the choice to either install a hoist or debilitate Sue, they surely would have chosen the hoist. On a cost basis alone, the hoist would have been the wiser decision. Sadly, many employers miss or ignore the subtle hints that offer the chance to prevent accidents. Some employers choose to dismiss them. Others simply don't know what to do.

Sue's back injury culminated from a number of shortsighted, poor judgments that placed employee welfare second to other considerations. First, Sue's request for a hoist upset the patient; a hoist installed above her bed would be a glaring sign of her progressing deterioration. While compassion for the patient was expected and reasonable, it did not warrant the risk placed on both hospital staff and the patient.

Second, after multiple requests did not produce the hoist, Sue completed a two-page form that was supposed to go straight to the director of nursing. Because the director happened to be on vacation, the assistant director decided to implement a make-shift solution, taking the wheels off the bed to lower the bed closer to the wheelchair height. This actually increased the hazard by making the bed lower than the wheelchair. Now, the patient had to be lifted up into the wheelchair rather than be lowered into it.

Third, Sue's employer knew that the patient's legs were unstable. Doctor's orders required Sue to get the patient out of bed at 6 a.m. when her legs were weak from the dormancy of sleep. It was exactly for this reason that the doctor ordered that the patient be moved so early. On the morning she was injured, Sue had two people helping her. "When a patient can pivot on their own power, only one person is needed. I had two helpers or I never would have done it." Clearly, people in charge knew of the safety risk involved.

The patient's collapse and the sudden distribution of her weight on Sue's neck were not the result of unforeseeable circumstances. The patient's fall was not beyond the employer's control; therefore, it could have been prevented. This "accident" was no accident. In light of the many ways Sue's injury could have been prevented, her loss seems all the worse.

Employers make decisions all the time that can affect people's health and welfare. When safety and health are not at the forefront of every such decision, 'accidents' build.

Sue says, "It was a big stink, me charting for three weeks that she needed a lift and her not wanting it. But I did not want her to get hurt either." She adds quietly, "I think she died from the Multiple Sclerosis she had."

Patients are fortunate to get nurses like Sue, not only experienced and competent but ones that genuinely care. No patient will receive Sue's nursing again. This too is a great and senseless loss.

Investing in Prevention

Good accident prevention pays off. According to OSHA, "establishing a safety and health program to prevent occupational injuries and illnesses is not only the right thing to do, it's the profitable thing to do. Studies have shown a $4 to $6 return for every dollar invested in safety and health."[10]

The fruits of accident prevention can be found by looking where OSHA focuses its attention. After employers receive an OSHA inspection and penalty, for instance, injuries and illnesses decrease an average of twenty-two percent within three years.[11] In OSHA's Voluntary Protection Program (VPP) where employers commit to integrating safety into their total management system, injury incident rates were 55 percent lower compared with similar industries.[12] All together in 1999, OSHA estimated that the VPP sites saved more than $130,000,000 in direct and indirect costs.[13]

In addition to preventing a tragedy, OSHA estimates that each avoided occupational fatality saves $910,000. Each prevented injury and illness that would have involved recovery time away from work saves $28,000. For each other serious injury and illness avoided, $7,000 is saved.[14]

Costs of injuries and illnesses include not only direct medical expenses and worker compensation, but also indirect costs, which can increase total costs by as much as four and a half times. Indirect costs include: training and paying replacement workers, investigating the accident, interrupted production, schedule delays, managing the claim, legal fees, and increased insurance costs. Considering both direct and indirect costs, OSHA gives the following illustrations to show how employers have to increase profit and sales just to recover from a direct $500 accident loss.

- a soft drink bottler would have to bottle and sell over 61,000 cans of soda

- a food packer would have to can and sell over 235,000 cans of corn

- a bakery would have to bake and sell over 235,000 donuts

- a contractor would have to pour and finish 3,000 square feet of concrete

- a ready-mix company would have to deliver 20 truckloads of concrete

- a paving contractor must lay 900 feet of two-lane asphalt road.[15]

One of the most important accident prevention ingredients is management commitment, but while many businesses eagerly jumped on quality programs to improve performance, many still neglect workplace health and safety. This is a mistake because preventing accidents is as fruitful and as manageable as quality control.

Like quality, occupational safety and health can be improved with systematic planning; teamwork; training; standard procedures; proper equipment, and adequate schedules and staffing. Since most of these factors are ultimately under management control, a founding tenet of occupational safety and health is that management holds ultimate responsibility for injury and illness prevention.

The "old days" of construction have been described like this: "In the early years of building construction, it was common practice to assume that accidents would claim one life for each two floors of a building, or for each million dollars of general construction work performed, or for each half-mile of tunnel construction. At that time, these numbers were actually put in the job estimate."[16] In other words, "Hey, accidents happen."

Regrettably, the cavalier approach towards safety is still the more prevalent, and successful efforts like OSHA's VPP are in the minority. According to OSHA, for example, only about 30 percent of businesses have even established comprehensive safety and health programs.[17] There is no federal OSHA standard requiring one.

***

Occupational injuries and illnesses occur in intolerable numbers, ruining lives and families and costing the nation nearly three-percent of gross domestic product.[18] They are preventable; therefore, it is logical to strongly address workplace health and safety as an important public health issue. This has not been done.

Because workplace accidents are mistakenly perceived as inevitable and uncontrollable happenings, they have not received the attention deserving of such a monumental cause of loss. The fact is, though, that most accidents are preventable. A paradigm shift, a change in the way we view workplace "accidents," is one of the steps required before the issue of occupational health and safety will be taken seriously. Another requisite paradigm shift involves misperceptions about injured workers.

CHAPTER 2

Salt in the Wound

The Stigma and the Reality of Workers' Compensation

A significant impediment to rousing support for occupational health and safety is the image of injured workers as scam artists; pot bellied middle age men lounging poolside tipping a beer; women with reported respiratory difficulties enjoying a cigarette; or fathers claiming back injuries while still able to lift their children.

Certainly, people faking injury or falsifying workers' compensation claims should be penalized, but those with legitimate claims should not be punished alongside them. Labeling all injured workers as frauds damages the esteem and image of people filing legitimate claims—the majority of people on workers' compensation. It makes their recovery that much harder.

The Myth of Workers' Compensation Fraud

In recent years, the insurance industry's focus on cheaters and malingerers helped push through national workers' compensation reform, a profitable cost-cutting campaign supported by outrage over alleged abuse of the system. The problem, however, is that the fraud image is false for the vast majority of workers' compensation cases. Studies show that only 1 to 2 percent of workers' compensation claims are fraudulent.[1][2] Certainly, the tens of thousands of workers killed every year were hardly aiming for a free ride on their employer's tab.

Jason Gunnett has literally seen both sides. While guiding a large piece of metal being moved by crane, Jason's hand was crushed so badly that it was almost amputated at the wrist. Once an injured construction laborer, Jason is now a degreed safety professional whose responsibilities include investigating occupational accidents.

"Even though I was a hard worker and was upset to learn I could not work for months, after a while, I got used to a new pattern of sleeping late and not sweating through a day of manual labor. My company had no light duty or return to work program and I definitely felt the temptation to avoid going back to work." Jason was fortunate that his pain was adequately controlled by medication, and due to his personal situation, he was able to comfortably manage through the financial loss.

Now a corporate industrial hygienist and safety engineer, Jason says, "You have to be a strong person to not become cynical regarding workers' compensation. Being a safety professional means you need to protect the employee first, and you have to investigate all reports of injury and illness with an open mind. Workers' compensation is hard to prove either way. There is no easy answer."

Even though the actual percentage of fraudulent cases is small, it is unacceptable and maddening for employers and those who manage compensation claims because it is so difficult to prove. The automatic and widespread suspicion of fraud, however, is unjustified and has grown so great that it taints almost all claims even though 98% are valid.

***

A national prime time television show aired a show on workers' compensation fraud, opening dramatically with footage of an old man working on a farm and a lawyer interviewing that same old man.

Announcer: This is DATELINE Monday, May 29th, 2000. Tonight. It's a crime that takes money out of your pocket, it starts with a lie.

Unidentified Lawyer: Are you able to lift anything?

Mr. Emil Mentel: A cup.

Lawyer: A cup?

Mr. Mentel: This is how I am.

Announcer: Think he's a broken old man? Here's what hidden cameras showed he was really doing while collecting money from you.

Mr. Manny Pageler: The man can grip. I see the legs working, I see the arms working.

John Larson reporting: When you first saw that videotape of him throwing that bale of hay, what was your reaction?

Mr. Pageler: I was mad.

Announcer: John Larson with lies, ripoffs and videotape.[3]

One of the many incendiary messages in this show is in the announcer's very first line when the viewer is informed that "money is taken right out of their pocket." Seconds later, the announcer again informs viewers that the supposedly injured man was throwing hay bales "while collecting money from you."

Money does not mysteriously float out of viewer's pockets as portrayed by the sensationalized lead into this segment. First, money paid to workers' compensation claims, including fraudulent ones, comes directly from insurance industry profits. Only after dipping into insurer profits does the cost get passed onto employers purchasing workers' compensation insurance. Then, the costs are spread over the entire group of policyholders; costs are not charged back to each employer dollar for dollar with their injuries. If employer rates do increase, the employer pays for it by one or more of the following ways: taking it out of the company profits; reducing wages; and passing it on to consumers. For the smaller number of companies that choose to self-insure, they pay the claims directly rather than pay premiums for workers' compensation insurance. Then, and only then, does it come out of the general public's pocket **IF** the public chooses to purchase the specific products made by companies with high workers' compensation rates. In neither case does money flow out of unsuspecting people's pockets as portrayed by the insurance industry.

The man featured in the NBC Dateline segment, Mr. Mentel, plead guilty to the felony charge of insurance fraud. He faked his disabilities and took advantage of both the workers' compensation system and a 74-year-old woman who gave him a job as an apartment manager. It was the worst of worst case scenarios. What made it such good drama was the fact that Mr. Mentel was an 80-year-old man who could apparently lie without shame and toss around 120-pound hay bales. On top of that, an insurance company investigator caught the shocking behavior on videotape.

Stone Phillips explained, "Because of his age, Emil Mentel was given no jail time. He was sentenced to five years probation and community service. He was also ordered to repay the insurance company the amount paid out on the claim, more than $118,000."

Instead of emphasizing the fact that a cheat was caught, the show furthered the perception that claimant fraud is a widespread form of art. For example, after introducing Frank Meyer, from the Sacramento district attorney's office, John Larson concludes: "...And Meyer promises the courts will continue to go after Workers' Compensation scam artists." Of course, the courts should prosecute wrongdoing, especially the intentional abuse of systems designed to help people. The real message here, however, is the threat of criminal prosecution. It is this threat that fosters under-reporting of legitimate claims and the overall shame of being an injured worker.

The rotten taste in the viewers mouth from a truly distasteful act is blurred with anger as the state prosecutor is allowed to say, "We want to send the message that these are serious offenses, that if you commit this kind of crime and get caught, that there's a good chance you will be prosecuted." It was like a commercial for the workers' compensation insurance industry and their anti-fraud campaign.

The show neglected to mention that in 1998, workers' compensation costs were only 1.35% of payroll down from a peak of 2.17% in 1993. It also failed to explain that between 1992 and 1998, workers' compensation costs to employers decreased 38% as a percentage of payroll while benefits to workers declined 35%.[4]

Instead, in the middle of the segment, reporter John Larson asserts, "After all, workers' compensation fraud is quite common. The industry estimates it adds up to $5 billion a year."[5] The American Federation of Labor and Congress of Industrial Organizations[6] (AFL-CIO) has heard this $5 billion claim before. The union's workers' compensation newsletter explained, "These allegations have absolutely no relationship to fact but are based on 'attitudes' about fraud (when respondents say they 'know' of someone supposedly on workers' comp even though he or she might be capable of working). A similar claim put workers' compensation fraud at 20 percent of the total of all claims in California in 1996; the truth was that suspected fraud that year, according to the state's Department of Insurance, was three-tenths of one percent!"[7]

In the summer of 2000, an independent team of experts—J. Paul Leigh, Ph.D., Steven Markowitz, M.D., Marianne Fahs, Ph.D., M.P.H., and Philip Landrigan, M.D.—published a book titled, "Costs of Occupational Injuries and Illnesses." In it, they estimated the national price tag for fraudulent claims to be 1.2 billion dollars, roughly one-fourth of the insurance industry estimate. Conceding that $1.2 billion is still a lot of money, the Leigh team put it into perspective by explaining that it was only about two-percent of all workers' compensation dollars spent in their sample year of 1994.[8] Whether the true fraud rate is less than one-percent or as high as two-percent, it is hardly "quite common."

The Dateline show provoked a response from the AFL-CIO Department of Occupational Health and Safety, which wrote:

> On May 29th NBC Nightly News and its program Dateline chose again to focus on an instance of worker fraud in workers' compensation. Despite the fact that studies show that claimant fraud in this system is minimal—in California, worker fraud is less that 3 tenths of 1 percent of all claims; and in Wisconsin, it is less than 1 tenth of 1 percent of claims, these exposés, encouraged by irresponsible allegations from the insurance industry, feed the myth that workers injured on the job are frauds, cheats, and malingerers.[9]

From the opposite side of the country, Robert Stern of the Washington State Labor Council, AFL-CIO also sent a letter to Dateline reporter Tom Brokaw. He received no response.

> Dear Mr. Brokaw:
>
> Approximately a week and a half ago, you broadcast a report on fraud by an injured worker in California. I frankly do not know whether or not this worker in fact committed fraud. I have no sympathy for workers who defraud the Industrial Insurance system. What is astonishing to me is that your report focused on what is acknowledged by the vast majority of academic experts to be, by far, the source of the lowest amount of fraud in the Industrial Insurance system. In every study that has been done on fraud in Workers' Compensation, employer, insurer, and provider fraud are found to be a dramatically greater problem than claimant fraud. At a time when injured workers throughout this nation are suffering enormously from "deform" of the system driven primarily by insurance providers, your report gave a seriously skewed presentation on the problems with the system.

I do not believe you have a serious interest in what is happening to injured workers, but if by chance you do, I urge you to take a look at the recommendations that were made by the National Commission on Workers' Compensation during the Nixon administration (an administration not particularly sympathetic to workers), then have your staff compare those recommendations to today's reality for injured workers. We should be ashamed of what we are doing to injured workers throughout this nation.

I wish I did not feel cynical about sending you this e-mail. I am sorry that you have bitten the insurance industry bait, hook, line and sinker."[10]

—Robert Stern, Special Assistant to the President,
Washington State Labor Council, AFL-CIO

In the 1970's, benefits to injured workers sunk so low that President Nixon appointed the National Commission on State Workmen's Compensation Laws to study the issue. It recommended that all states pay totally disabled workers at least two-thirds of their salary up to a maximum of the state's average weekly wage. Still, 17 states have not complied with the Commission's recommended standard wage.[11]

Studies support Stern's assertion that employer fraud is much greater than claimant fraud. In Florida, a 1995-1996 compliance audit found that of 22,758 employers contacted, 13.1% were operating without legally required worker's compensation insurance. In just the next year, the auditors found the rate grew another half percent.[12] Stating that 13.6% is probably an underestimate, the audit report explained that in addition to the large number of employers making no attempt to buy the insurance, still others cheat the system by intentionally under-reporting or misclassifying its payroll and by falsely representing employees as independent contractors.[13]

In a 1997 press release, the Wisconsin Department of Workforce Development stated that workers' compensation fraud in the state was less than six-tenths of one percent.[14] As recently as November 1, 2000, the same department reported on fraud from 1994 to 1999 concluding, "The public perception of workers' compensation fraud is exaggerated," and "The documented level of workers' compensation fraud in Wisconsin is minimal."[15]

A few months after the Dateline show aired, the LA Times printed, "Anti-Fraud Drive Proves Costly for Employees," and found, "Over the last decade, employers and insurance carriers have saved billions of dollars as legislatures in many states rolled back benefits, more narrowly defined workplace injuries and introduced impediments to collecting for them."[16]

And the J. Paul Leigh team concluded, "The dollar amount of fraudulent workers' compensation claims submitted by workers pales in comparison to the amount for claims never filed and, more importantly, the overall small amount of total costs paid by workers' compensation systems. Moreover, fraud committed by insurance companies at workers' expense is likely to be significant."[17]

The Leigh team further estimated that workers' compensation covers only 27 percent of all occupational illness and injury costs and that taxpayers bear a financial burden of 28.5 billion dollars —close to six times the estimate of workers' compensation fraud—through Medicare, Medicaid, and Social Security. Further, they discovered that costs were borne by injured workers and their families, by all workers through lower wages, by employers with lower profits and by consumers with higher prices. Specifically, they estimated that injured and ill workers and their families absorbed about 44% of the costs.[18] Now that is injustice worthy of outrage.

***

Where Are the Benefits?
Fraud is committed in order to gain something. For most

people on workers' compensation, there is no reward, financial or otherwise. Indeed, most suffer financial loss.

Workers' compensation benefits include partial replacement of lost wages, medical expenses and survivor benefits for dependents, but for most injured or ill workers, the system costs them money from day one. Benefits like overtime or use of a company car are lost. Depending on the state, workers have to wait 3-7 days before receiving payment. If the insurance company denies the claim, an appeal to the state workers' compensation board can take anywhere from 30 days in Michigan to 1.5 years in Iowa.[19] No payments are received in the meanwhile.

In August of 2000, researchers at the non-profit Rand institution reported that workers from the largest firms in California that filed for permanent partial disabilities received $19,000 in workers' compensation benefits but lost an average of $39,500 in wages. The report also found that, for many claimants, workers' compensation benefits failed to meet the common standard to replace two-thirds of the workers pre-tax dollars.[20]

California is one of the states that does not comply with the recommendation from the National Commission on State Workmen's Compensation Laws to provide up to 200% of the state's average weekly wage. Instead, the maximum payment is 66% of the state's average weekly wage. (Workers earning less than the average weekly wage receive 66% of their actual earnings.) Californians temporarily disabled on the job, therefore, receive a maximum benefit of $490 per week even if their income was much higher than that prior to the injury or illness. In other words, workers are not compensated for income over $38,258. Even worse, workers temporarily disabled in New York receive only 48% of the state's average weekly wage—a maximum of $400 per week. New Yorkers, therefore, are not compensated for incomes over $31,231. Only one state, Iowa, has complied with the 30-year-old National Commission's recommendation to provide 200% of the state's average weekly wage, a maximum benefit of $1,031.[21]

Stranger than the disparity between state disability benefits is the value allocated to permanent disabilities. If a worker cuts their hand off in Pennsylvania, it's worth $228,620. A worker suffering the same fate in Washington, however, would receive only $6,572. Nationally, the average benefit for a lost hand is $94,734.[22] The state you happen to work in, however, makes all the difference.

Regardless of how good the policy, private health insurance is not responsible for workplace injuries or illnesses. That's why dental and medical claim forms have a little check box next to the standard question, "Is this claim related to a workplace accident?" If the yes box is checked, they can and will deny the claim.

In addition to the financial loss, there are other drawbacks to being on workers' compensation. For example, workers filing for workers' compensation forfeit their medical privacy, and have little, if any, choice in medical care. Many are followed and investigated by private detectives. Some companies have policies where they automatically use a private investigator, for instance, on every back injury with ten days out of work or randomly on ten percent of all claims. One injured worker explained how upsetting it was to sit in a courtroom and find photos of her walking her daughter to school, an activity that revealed nothing about her claim.

Marlys Harris wrote a report for the non-profit Consumer Reports magazine and summarized the national workers' compensation situation this way: "Workers deserve more help from the workers' compensation system than they're getting."[23] Similar to the Leigh team's findings, Harris also concluded that inadequately cared for injured workers cost taxpayers money when they have to file for Social Security or public assistance.[24]

After publishing the report, Harris explained her perception on why injured workers are poorly treated. She said, "The population of injured workers is small and unorganized. People distrust the issue and it is hard to get them to see it."

She elaborated, "The insurance companies admit that workers were injured but then they refer to the long-term, ongoing problems as symptom exaggeration. It's insidious. I even found myself wondering if I was being taken. Acknowledging the initial injury and then saying it is the employee's fault for not going back to work does make you suspicious. It is hard to combat."[25]

The President and CEO of the National Council on Compensation Insurance, Inc., Bill Schrempf, wrote a letter to Consumer Reports expressing disapproval of the report. Calling it one-sided, Mr. Schrempf listed the changes generally sought by workers' compensation reform as:

- Root out fraud
- Improve return-to-work incentives
- Improve the equity and delivery of benefit payments
- Reduce attorney involvement[26]

But the very four workers' compensation changes that Mr. Schrempf lists come from slicing the injured workers' piece of the pie that much thinner. His list, intended to balance the issue, instead confirms how injured and ill workers ultimately pay for the cost cutting.

Mr. Schrempf goes on to say that as a result of workers' compensation reform, "fewer workers are being injured or killed on the job." While businesses and insurance companies have no doubt saved money from workers' compensation reform, taking credit for anything more—especially accident reduction—is quite a stretch of the imagination. His goals say nothing about improving accident prevention. If anything, the fear of criminal prosecution and the stigma associated with the "injured worker" image reduced claims not by preventing injuries but by preventing the reporting of those injuries.

There are innumerable reasons why workers don't want to file for workers' compensation. Many sincerely do not want to burden their employers so they cope with injuries and illnesses on their own, seeing their regular doctors and using sick days if they need to. Some ignore their problems until they become unbearable, costing more suffering and money in the long run. Many fear the threat of criminal prosecution, like the one clearly made on the NBC Dateline show, if they cannot prove their injury or illness occurred at work. At companies with safety incentive programs, injured workers can not only ruin the company and department safety record but they can also cost their bosses and co-workers rewards like money, time off with pay or the prestige of a safety award.

Todd O'Malley is an attorney that knows the system. He is founder and partner of O'Malley & Langan, an East Coast law firm representing injured and ill workers; chairman of the workers' compensation section of the Association of Trial Lawyers of America; and Board member of the Workplace Injury Litigation Group, a national non-profit organization of attorneys representing injured workers.

One of his clients had his foot run over by a forklift. O'Malley explains, "It looks like a football. It is huge and discolored and he can't wear any shoes. This guy is so ashamed that he leaves his window blinds drawn so his neighbors don't see him doing anything. One day I asked him, 'What could they possibly see you do? You can't do anything anyway!' He told me, 'Sometimes I hobble around just to do some stuff.' So, here is a guy with a huge, purple foot so big that you can't possibly miss it. He is hobbling around in his own house, and he is still ashamed to be an injured worker."

O'Malley concludes, "The perception of injured workers as scams is even held by injured workers. One injured worker once said to me, 'It's too bad all the frauds ruined it for legitimate people.' That is the problem in a nutshell—there is no 'all the frauds.'"

The Real Fraud

The outrage over workers' compensation fraud is misdirected at workers when it should be focused on cheating employers, says Greg Tarpinian, Executive Director of Labor Research Associates, a New York City-based non-profit research and advocacy organization that provides research and educational services for trade unions. He reports, "The best evidence from the states that have pursued fraud and generated detailed records indicates that for every $1 lost in claimant fraud, at least $4 to $5 (and in some states as much as $10) are lost through premium fraud. Premium fraud includes a number of schemes used by employers to reduce the workers' compensation insurance premiums by underreporting payroll, misclassifying employees' occupations and misrepresenting their claims experience."[27]

Both intentional and unintentional underreporting on the employer's part occurs. One injured worker explained that when he needed a few stitches, his employer told him, "Just go see your own doctor and bring us the bill." The bill was directly paid from petty cash, and the injury was not reported.[28]

If injuries and illnesses are not reported, they are not paid for by workers' compensation. One finding from the National Institute of Occupational Safety and Health (NIOSH) SEN-SOR program, a collaborative effort with 13 State health departments to improve occupational health, discovered that state health departments in Michigan, New Jersey, and Washington State ".... demonstrated gross underutilization of workers' compensation for occupational illnesses: less than 43 percent of workers with silicosis and only 25 percent of workers with occupational dermatitis filed for compensation."[29] Dermatitis is one of the most common work-related illnesses and silicosis is one of the oldest and deadliest.

The Institute of Medicine (part of the congressionally chartered National Academy of Sciences) assembled a panel of experts and published *Safe Work in the 21st Century*; it reported that as much as 30 - 60 percent of work related *fatalities* are not included in workers' compensation records.[30] These respected and valid studies don't make national news shows yet the dollars at stake exceed even the highest estimates of workers' compensation fraud. Why? Because the bills are paid by the injured, the ill, and the taxpayer.

For those that have filed for workers' compensation, benefits are hardly guaranteed. Denying payment is a common ploy by insurance companies because it is so difficult for sick people to fight. Many patients give up seeking payment for all or at least some of their bills and pay them directly—to argue over each one is too difficult. Called "starving them out," this tactic often brings workers and their families—already suffering from an injury or illness—the added burdens of depression; stress; financial loss or devastation; divorce; drinking and even suicide. One injured worker was actually told by an insurer "not to take it personally. It's just part of the game."[31]

Sue got so mad once at how her employer's workers' compensation carrier routinely denied her medical bills that she went to court with a 104 degree fever to show she was sick from the MRSA infection. She says, "Even the judge was disgusted with how the insurance company dragged me into court again and again."

Sue tries hard to not be bullied by her employer's workers' compensation insurance company. They attempted to terminate her benefits, but she sued and had them reinstated. She has gone to about 30 hearings in the last two years, once to fight a denial for a $3.82 prescription.

Sue describes her finances this way. "Workers' compensation only pays me a percentage of my wages to begin with. Then my lawyers take another chunk every two weeks, there are no cost of living increases (I was injured in 1994), bonuses or overtime;

and now they want part of my pension." Although she is eligible, Sue refuses to file for her pension because the insurance company is allowed to deduct the employer-contributed part from her compensation check. This is all in addition to repeated starve-out tactics and denials for medical bill payment.

Sue's is not an isolated case. Brian is a 24-year veteran printer living in Iowa with his wife and three kids. He has permanent neurological damage from solvent exposure. Some of his symptoms are: confusion, fatigue, insomnia, anxiety and depression, peripheral vision loss, upper body tremors, headache and swollen eyelids. Permanently disabled and chemically sensitized, Brian received a lump-sum settlement of $50,000.

"One of the workers' compensation doctors called me a malingerer. I knew this wasn't something good so I went home and looked it up. It means 'feigning an illness for monetary gain.' So I sent him my test results that showed a 30% loss of brain function and asked him how $50,000 was worth 30% of my brain. I made that much every year."

Although Brian's medical diagnosis is toxic encephalopathy, an industrial illness, his workers' compensation claim was denied. He explains, "When they pay you off, the claim is denied. They denied it all the way — I even went to California for a PET (positron emission tomography) scan and they denied it. My wife's insurance company paid, and if they approved my claim, they would have had to reimburse her carrier for the medical expenses."

Brian was never particularly interested in the small print on the chemicals he worked with day-in and day-out for over two decades. He said, "It was just part of my job. If you're a painter, you work around paint. If you're a printer, you work around solvents. We all used it that way, twice a day for 15 minutes each time. I didn't know it would cost me 30% of my brain. I am a lot smarter now with 30% less of my brain."

In Oregon, Ernie Delmazzo also learned about workplace

safety and health the hard way. For ten weeks, he drove a truck 1,300 to 1,800 miles each week. He describes the drive like "riding a mechanical bull, being bounced forward and backward for 8 to 14 hours a day." The suspension was shot but the truck rental company gave his employer a great rate on the lease.

When an MRI was done four months later, delayed by a claim denial, Ernie's doctors recommended immediate surgery on his neck. They said any fall or slip could cause him to become a quadriplegic. Even so, it took two years and two months to get surgery, delayed by a second claim denial. Ernie says, "If I ever get in a car accident, the car insurer could deny the claim saying it's work-related. The workers' compensation insurer would probably also deny the claim because the injury would be old and partially related to a car accident. So, taxpayers will pay and I could end up penniless and paralyzed."

In his current state, Ernie is considered 21% disabled. For his disability, he received a lifetime benefit of $8,500. At one point, it took seven months before he received any wage replacement and over a year before his doctors were paid.

Ernie's treatment so outraged him that he co-founded Injured Workers' Alliance, a grassroots organization dedicated to educating the public, helping injured workers and improving the workers' compensation system. Its website, www.injuredworker.org is a great place for an injured or ill worker to begin helping themselves.

Even health care workers are not immune from workplace injuries and illnesses. After twenty years in nursing, Angela went into a storage room during a transplant operation for supplies, and had to reach over six big nitrogen containers and a box on the floor to get them. She fell, hit her head, herniated three discs in her neck, and tore her rotator cuff and a bicep tendon.

The self-insured, Florida hospital she worked for did not compensate her for the first six weeks she could not work. They also did not compensate her six months later when she was declared permanently disabled. As a single mother with two kids in college, Angela could not afford to lose her paychecks. Finally, Angela accepted $14,000 in back pay when she was owed $24,000. By then, she was desperate. She lost her house, $20,000 in equity, and her car.

Eventually, Angela had to move back in with her parents. She explained, "At 47 years old, I had to live with my parents for a year. I was ashamed to tell them. It was so demeaning, even though they were wonderful."

At one point, Angela was so depressed she became suicidal. She explained, "I would probably be dead if not for my lawyer. You have to fight for everything. I am into this three-years now, and if I start to think about it, I cry. It is so frustrating. I am doing better but I have to rebuild entirely."

No sane person voluntarily takes these torturous paths looking for quick and easy financial gain. There is no incentive for it, financial or otherwise.

Exclusive Remedy

Workers' compensation is hardly the gold mine insurers portray it as. Fat lawsuits and big settlements are usually completely out of the question.

"When I tell distraught families who just lost someone in a workplace fatality that they cannot sue the employer, they are shocked. Sometimes it takes attorneys to tell them the same thing until they believe it," says Ron Hayes, founder of Families in Grief Hold Together (The FIGHT Project). "I've had families go to three or four attorneys until they would accept it. It depends on how angry they are."

The National Academy of Social Insurance, a private, non-profit, non-partisan resource center explains the workers' compensation arrangement this way:

"Under the exclusive remedy concept, the worker accepts workers' compensation as payment in full, without recourse to an additional tort suit. Employers are responsible for benefit payments as prescribed by workers' compensation laws, thereby ending their liability."[32]

In other words, exclusive remedy safeguards employers from large punitive awards but impedes justice in the many cases that might be better served in court. The bottom line is that in all but the most willfully negligent circumstances, injured and ill workers cannot sue their employer for making them injured or ill.

Discussing exclusive remedy in an online article, the law firm of Boxer & Gerson explained a California case this way:

"The survivors of three workers killed by the Tosco refinery explosion were awarded a total of $21 million in damages. The workers were *not* employees of Tosco but of a subcontractor at the site; thus they had the right to sue Tosco for negligence. In contrast, Steve Duncan was a Tosco employee. He survived by jumping off the tower while ablaze from the blast. His sole remedy is workers' compensation. As a result of falling some 60 feet, Duncan broke almost every bone in his body. He has had 24 surgeries to date, numerous skin grafts, and amputation of his fingers and a thumb on one hand. He is confined to a wheelchair; and has numerous metal pins sticking out from his knee and thigh.

He was earning more than $1,000 per week. Now, he gets $490 a week in temporary disability benefits. Even if he is totally, permanently disabled, this is the most he will ever get—no cost of living raise and no lump sum payment. If he is found to be less than 100% permanently disabled—even if marginally less, such as 99.75% disabled—he will receive just $230 week in permanent disability benefits—and not for life, but for a finite period of time.[33]

Hayes explains, "In a handful of states, there are certain exceptions that let people sue, such as when a person behaves criminally. But usually, they cannot sue their direct employer. Instead, they have to sue other employers that were involved (like on a multi-employer construction site) or they can sue under product liability, like when someone killed by a drill rig sues the manufacturer of the equipment rather than the employer who did not maintain it or train workers on it."

"But," cautions Ron, "what people don't realize is that if they win these lawsuits, they then have to return all money received under workers' compensation because winning the suit will actually prove someone else was at fault. So here are these families that fight to win in court and then they discover that of any award they received, they have to pay the lawyers 30-40% off the top, return any workers' compensation they have received back to the insurance company (sometimes a lump sum of $20,000 or more) and they won't receive any more payments under workers' compensation. The employer's insurance company actually ends up getting their money back." Ron describes the whole mess, saying "It's like the lawyers need to hire economists to figure out if the families will end up with anything."

A frustrated medical doctor vented to her local newspaper, writing not about the struggle to heal but about the battle that forces many of her patients to seek legal help.

Letter published in "The Oklahoman," March 12, 2000:

To the Editor:

I've worked for the past nine years as the "company doctor" for many businesses in Oklahoma. In my experience, 90 to 95 percent of workers simply want to get well and get back to work. They are frightened of retribution and loss of their jobs. Many times they do lose their jobs right after they return to full duty. This is supposed to be illegal, but it happens every day. I've fought with companies to get adequate care for these people; it's an uphill battle. Very few start with an attorney. Here is why they go to an attorney with a workers' compensation injury.

- They don't receive their pay for a month or more and no one

at the company "knows anything about it."
- They are doing light duty, the supervisor refuses to follow the restrictions and the company won't enforce it.
- The supervisor and other employees are allowed to harass and ridicule the employee who is on light duty.
- They are refused the treatment their doctor recommends.

It's sad when someone had worked for a company for 20 years with excellent reviews but becomes a pariah when injured. Wise up, governor. Some companies care nothing about the Oklahomans who work for them.[34]

—Melissa Smith-Horn

The flip side of the exclusive remedy coin is that workers are paid even if an injury was partially their fault. If a person missteps and falls off a ladder, for instance, he or she is still compensated. The exclusive remedy trade-off works for many short duration injuries and illnesses where the system achieves the goal of prompt compensation without lawsuits. For most seriously injured and ill workers, however, the system does not work fairly.

After lengthy investigation, Executive Director Greg Tarpinian from Labor Research Associates concludes, "The presumption of widespread malingering and dishonesty undercuts any meaningful discussion of the adequacy of benefits and provides a convenient response for those opposed to the benefit increases that are so critically needed in many states. Until the misplaced focus on claimant fraud is overcome, district attorneys will continue to fry the small fish while the big fish go free, and the voting public will remain distracted by anecdotes. The emphasis on fraud and costs also distracts the public and lawmakers from the workplace hazards and flagrant safety violations that are the real cause of the problem of worker injuries and workers' compensation costs."[35]

***

"There are things that can be done better," says industrial

hygienist Jason Gunnett. He suggests, "Employers are better off taking a proactive approach and controlling workplace hazards instead of blaming employees after accidents happen. By focusing on prevention—things like hazard identification, safety controls, and training—companies reduce their exposure. Most importantly, proactive safety programs focus on risk—they look ahead to prevent accidents instead of looking back."

He continues, "I don't believe we'll ever eliminate all workers' compensation fraud, but if an employer controls hazards and sets guidelines, workers will have no structured basis for a fraudulent case. Some employers don't even investigate accidents but they should—they should take it one step further and investigate near misses to make every attempt to avoid accidents in the first place. Employers without structured safety programs like these will have higher workers' compensation rates."

The painful toll of work-related illnesses and injuries is beyond measure. For injured and ill workers, it has become acceptable to assume guilt until proven innocent, burdening them with an indignity that is cruel, chronic and unjust.

It is wrong to judge and penalize entire populations for the failings of a few. That is stereotyping. The image of fraudulent malingerers, while appropriate for a small minority, does not reflect the reality of post-injury/illness life for more than 98% of workers' compensation claimants. The injured worker stigma not only harms injured and ill workers further, it damages the nation by obscuring the subject of occupational health and safety and hindering meaningful public discussion about serious problems in the workers' compensation system.

Because there is no national regulation of workers' compensation, each state runs its own program. Without enforceable guidelines to keep the playing field fair and level, states compete for new business by pushing the overhead costs of workers' compensation lower and lower, even advertising their rates to draw new industry. Likewise, the insurance industry manages claims under a microscope to increase profits. The result: today's workers' compensation system is nothing more than a manipulative business expense.

The Other America

The classic 'American Dream' rests on the dignity and pride of being able to make something of oneself. We ask our children "What do you want to be when you grow up?" because we believe that, with hard work, they can be whatever they want to be. We don't tell them that if they get injured or ill while pursuing that dream, all bets are off.

In addition to the physical pain, financial hardship and the loss of their self-image as self-sufficient members of their families and society, injured and ill workers are essentially discarded. They are outcasts. With the exception of the elderly and young, America shows little mercy for those who cannot work, those "permanently disabled" from a workplace injury or illness.

In June of 2000, at a chapter meeting of the Pennsylvania Federation of Injured Workers, an announcement was made concerning an upcoming Labor Day parade. The local chapter president thought a float in the parade would raise awareness of the plight of injured workers. The room fell silent when he asked for volunteers; only proud people march in parades. The insurance industry's campaign to root out fraud had been heard.

Tim Wagner was Executive Director of the Pennsylvania Federation of Injured Workers for five years, until it was forced to close its doors due to lack of funding. He described the indignity this way. "The America you knew before you were injured is not the America you know afterwards. The rights and privileges people think they have before they are injured dissolves afterwards. You go from being a productive member of society to being seen and treated as a bum."

When he took the organization's lead in 1995, Tim was an ordained Lutheran minister. His decision cost him his ordination and half his salary. About his choice, he says, "This is the hardest job I've ever done. Insurers have done a good job of showing injured workers as lazy malingerers. The fraud image is so powerful that even the unions and the workers themselves buy into it. People suspect their co-workers of milking the system and this pits employers and employees together against the injured worker."

Tim explains, "Most injured workers enter the workers' compensation system reluctantly but they have no other choice. Co-workers become pawns of the insurance industry when they don't support the injured. It's divide and conquer. "

Most people who work would not voluntarily assume the indignity, isolation and stigma of unemployment. Recipients of workers' compensation *are people who were working in the first place*. It is illogical to assume they are all seeking to scam the system.

Sue did not work for three weeks with a broken neck because it was easy to leave her job, because she wanted to stay home and watch Oprah. She still says "If I could go to work for even just five minutes a day, I would do it." Today, her self-image reflects the new reality of her life—she can no longer do the things she wants to do. Sue started counseling to help handle the grief and to learn to cope, paying for it herself.

From her daughter's poem, more "Tears..."

> Although disabled through her injury; she seeks truth
> and justice;
> Searching for the answer that has been denied her.
> The people who were set to help her further her decline
> deeper;
> The workers' compensation group fuels lies and deceit
> here.

Six years after her neck broke, a school bus lightly rear-ended their car as Sue sat inside with her son. While her son barely moved, Sue's brittle neck fractured immediately.

Her current condition is so severe that doctors can only prescribe "pain management"— another way of saying, "There is nothing we can do for you." Instead of healing others, Sue's job now is to get through each day with the constant pain of a fractured neck and several loose, broken bone pieces floating near-by. "Not to mention managing my claim," she says, "which is a full time job in itself."

Living with a fractured neck, Sue's pain management prescription is no aspirin. Her pills cost $180 per month. Again, the workers' compensation insurance company is trying to terminate her benefits claiming they are not responsible for her current condition since it was the bus that caused her neck to fracture.

In response to this recent round of 'starve out' tactics, Sue paid for the $180 dollar prescription herself until she could no longer afford it. Fuming, she grits out, "It is their responsibility. Normal people don't fracture their necks at 5-miles-per-hour but mine is so bad that if someone slapped me on the back, it could break."

When Sue tells her local pharmacies that the prescription is related to a workers' compensation claim, they ask her who will pay. Sue says, "They laugh at me when I tell them who the insurance company is. I can't even get this prescription filled unless I pay for it myself because the pharmacies know that the bill will be denied."

At only 13-years-old, Sue's daughter has already seen "the other America." In "Tears," she wrestles with what to believe after seeing how her mother is treated.

> "Reaching out to others, who may help or not, to hear her story upon deaf ears;
> The people who were elected in by the people; turning their noses.
> The constitution reads, "We the People" which I assumed was written for the people.
> I come to find those words have no meaning, they are in jest for no purposes.
> Our lawmakers forgot about the Constitution of the United States;
> They choose to represent those of great wealth.

Our forefathers stood for equal rights of the common
man;
Not to buckle into Corporations with their non-ethical
stealth.

After watching her mother's slow physical decay, witnessing
the disrespect of the system, living with the hardship of having
a disabled mom, and sharing the family's financial loss, Sue's
daughter closes "Tears" with mercy and hope.

I pray each evening to bring one day free of pain
for my mother;
To pray for these immoral people's souls and ask
that they be forgiven.
I pray that someone will listen to the pain, agony,
frustration of other workers;
That the Lord above will answer my prayers and be
acted upon by heaven.

CHAPTER 3

Non-Discriminating Risk

The General Public

Many people still picture workers as either "white collar workers" or "blue collar workers." The blue-collar image is usually one of uniformed factory workers or construction laborers. White collar workers, on the other hand, are pictured in offices surrounded by papers and computers. Traditionally, white collar workers had formal educations while blue collar workers were skilled in the trades. A slang description was that white collar workers earned a living with their brains and blue collar workers earned theirs with their hands. In the past, workplace safety and health was primarily a blue-collar issue.

Today, all kinds of workers face occupational threats, not just blue collar workers. We are in a new millennium where old worker stereotypes no longer apply. Today's general public consists of all types of workers, and each will play a critical role if workplace health and safety are to be improved.

Office work is often assumed to be non-hazardous simply because it takes place in an office. Commonly, however, unmanaged office environments become polluted by the people inhabiting them, by uninvited guests like spore-releasing molds, and by familiar office equipment like copiers and printers. Problems like overcrowding, inadequate fresh air intake, and poor building maintenance can be found even in the most posh office buildings. And, when offices share building space or ventilation systems with industrial workplaces, the air in the office can be the same as that in the nearby manufacturing facility, shipping department, laboratory or warehouse.

Indoor air quality is the perfect example of a workplace hazard that holds no stereotypes. Regardless of how fancy the office or the status of the people inside, poor indoor air quality can make them sick.

For six years, Sarah worked in the marketing department at an equipment manufacturer's corporate headquarters in Minnesota. Hired as a secretary, she gradually earned the title of Marketing Services Coordinator as her skills grew. A bright and ambitious 34-year-old, she had no reason to suspect she was slowly being poisoned by the air she breathed.

Sarah worked for six years before her symptoms began: muscle aches, headaches, facial swelling, hoarseness in her throat, and coughing. She was diagnosed with the amorphous illness of fibromyalgia and no connection was made between her condition and her workplace. That is, until a new marketing promotion started.

About the time of her fibromyalgia diagnosis, white advertising balloons were distributed to company vendors as part of a promotion campaign. The marketing staff tied some up in their office and later noticed they were beginning to yellow. The staff then saw the balloons become sticky and blotched and puckered in places.

As the appearance worsened, Sarah and her co-workers assumed something must be wrong with the balloons. Worried the balloons would present a shoddy company image, they quickly contacted their dealers, but none reported yellowing. Only the floating balloons in the marketing department at corporate headquarters had changed. They realized that whatever was affecting the balloons came from the air inside their office.

Since then, Sarah discovered that she and her co-workers were exposed to degreasing chemicals from a print shop down the hall. She learned that the air handling systems were shared; not enough fresh air was drawn in; and air from the print shop was being sucked into the offices through a rusty heat exchanger. The heat exchanger accelerated the chemical breakdown—a process known as oxidation—and dispersed chemicals into the offices that were as toxic and possibly more toxic than those used in the print shop. This was the sticky stuff yellowing and puckering the balloons.

After Sarah notified her employer, the company performed some general air monitoring. Unsatisfied by the response, Sarah used her own money and hired an independent, consulting toxicologist to tell her what kicked her immune system into overdrive and left her with a debilitating case of multiple chemical sensitivity. He concluded that although her body now responds to many chemicals with an exaggerated immune response, it started with a low level, long-term exposure to oxides of a chemical used in the print shop. The mystery of Sarah's life-altering chemical allergy was solved and its name was d-limonene.

Sarah now has a huge medical file filled with reports like the one that says, "Aliphatic volatile solvent test of adipose tissue specimen shows 160-ppb n-hexane." A brain scan for toxic encephalopathy (brain damage from chemical exposure) is riddled with spooky findings like "mismatch between the early and late phases, salt and pepper pattern and shunting to the soft tissues, which are part of a pattern seen in patients with neurotoxic exposure."

Despite her history of office work, Sarah's medical summary concludes, "The prognosis for this condition is poor. I have seen a large number of patients with chemical sensitivities in the past, and, when patients have this degree of disability, recovery is unlikely."

In her daily life, the complex chemical formulas and strange medical terms translate into very real limitations for Sarah and her family. Her neurological damage often makes her confused and she sometimes misplaces things. "I feel disorganized all the time but I know it is just the brain damage. "She has eye twitches and her top lip occasionally goes numb. Sarah is so sensitized to chemicals that if a waitress spray-cleans a nearby table, she becomes ill with a headache and nausea and often has to leave. On her husband's birthday recently, Sarah and her family were able to go to a restaurant because they purposefully went late in the evening. "We have better odds of getting a table away from the other diners. Ladies often put on more perfume when they go out to dinner and the chemicals in the perfume will make me sick."

In addition to Sarah's fierce chemical allergy from the oxides of d-limonene, she suffers nervous system damage from yet another chemical. "3-methyl-2-hexanone" was the answer when Sarah's employer sent a sticky balloon from the marketing department along with an unused balloon to a laboratory and asked, "What is the difference?" The laboratory report noted the bizarre request and recommended, "If the sticky substance is still an issue, a study using series test balloons handled in a controlled manner should be done." In other words, testing should be done properly.

Instead of conducting a better "balloon" study or performing air sampling for 3-methyl-2-hexanone, the employer chose to take only general screening-type air samples. When these detected no obvious problems, they assumed that there was no health problem instead of responding with a new sampling approach aggressive enough to find the cause of Sarah's illness. Despite lab reports indicating their presence, the employer never sampled for d-limonene products or 3-methyl-2-hexanone so Sarah has no way to definitively prove her illness was caused by her workplace. The best proof she has is that a qualified toxicologist said, "On the basis of information that I have been provided, I conclude that sufficient reason exists to implicate "occupational exposure to chemicals" as the cause of Sarah's disability."

Because office work is assumed to be clean, workers often have difficulty getting employers to believe there may be a health concern. Most office environments do not routinely undergo air monitoring or safety and health inspections, making hazards more likely to go undetected. Many companies with office-type workplaces don't even have health and safety staff to investigate concerns or complaints.

The prevalence of poor indoor air quality (IAQ), for example, has increased since the 1970's when energy conservation encouraged tighter buildings. Also called "Sick Building Syndrome," all types of buildings are susceptible. The EPA's own employees have complained of poor indoor air quality caused by carpeting and poor ventilation. The agency once shut down its own day-care center for high carbon monoxide levels from diesel exhaust sucked into the ventilation system from a mall parking garage and a nearby tunnel.[1]

Lots of things can cause poor IAQ . Sources include manufacturing chemicals; chemicals released from carpets, furniture, or other building materials; chemicals brought in by co-workers like perfumes or, ironically, air fresheners; biological organisms like molds and bacteria; tobacco smoke; outside air pollution brought inside; or from mechanical equipment like copiers, printers, forklift trucks, etc. Inadequate fresh air intake and overcrowding are common contributors to unhealthy indoor air.

Typical IAQ-related symptoms include: headaches, fatigue, burning or itching eyes, nasal congestion, coughing and dry throats, nasal congestion and nausea. Making matters worse, IAQ symptoms mimic other illnesses and can change week to week or even day to day. They are difficult to prove since symptoms are felt; they are not visible like a broken bone or a skin rash.

Sarah has stacks of emails telling her employer of her symptoms and concern. She kept trusting them, waiting for them to fix things. The employer had an in-house safety department and a certified industrial hygiene consultant; the company could have easily sampled properly. Instead, they chose to stop looking. The Minnesota Department of Labor and Industry took the same path. Sarah even found the Hazard Evaluation and Technical Assistance Branch in NIOSH and requested a formal health hazard evaluation. They responded with an "informational letter." No one believed Sarah.

Initially, the company doctor diagnosed Sarah with fibromyalgia and sinusitis. Two private doctors recommended that she not return to work, one commented that her "immune system was sensitized to broad classifications of chemicals and she has become frankly allergic to them." After four months on medical leave, Sarah was fired. With her workers compensation claim denied from the beginning, Sarah and her husband cashed in their savings to pay for medical and legal bills. They went from anticipating a comfortable retirement to owing back taxes.

Sarah fears for the health of the co-workers she left behind. One of her co-workers showed three of the same chemicals in her blood as were found in Sarah's—chemicals found in industrial environments. Hardly a fly-by-night organization, Sarah's ex-employer is a well-known name brand with 4,700 employees worldwide.

***

Mike McGuinness is a Certified Industrial Hygienist (CIH) and President of RK Occupational & Environmental Analysis Inc. in Phillipsburg, New Jersey. He is one of the few CIHs (less than one percent) also board certified in the specialty of Indoor Environmental Quality. After investigating thousands of indoor air quality complaints, "Most of them," he says, "involve mold contamination."

In his classes, Mike tells his students, "After twenty years, I've learned that a clean, dry building is better than a wet and dirty building. Good indoor air quality is simple—design and maintain the ventilation system properly and control moisture. In most cases, that is enough to prevent poor air quality from ever developing."

And yet many shortsighted building owners and operators continue to skimp on preventative maintenance. Once contamination is allowed to build to the point where workers feel ill, things get complicated and costly. Microbes, for example, can be successfully killed but the dead bodies are often as allergenic as the live ones; they serve as organic "food" for the next generation of microbes to feed on. Cleaning indoor environments of microbes often involves enclosing the entire work area in plastic, filtering the exhaust air, sampling, and providing clean-up workers with respirators and protective clothing. Normal business operations are shut down until final sampling shows acceptable results.

People with asthma, severe allergies, sinusitis, immune suppression or chronic inflammatory lung diseases are especially susceptible to indoor air quality problems. After spending so much time poking through buildings with poor air quality, Mike has personally become sensitized to the some of the molds and chemicals that he is hired to find. "I go into some of these buildings and I know I should put on a respirator," he says, "but the people inside would panic and I'd probably get fired. So when I have to, I return at night and wear a respirator."

Mike finds that many building owners disregard IAQ until people do something drastic like picket or call the press. "It doesn't make sense," he says. "Building owners are motivated by cost but they don't realize that sick buildings cost them money in absenteeism, lawsuits, broken leases, and reduced productivity. Healthy buildings are not only better for the workers, they save money. In the long run, it costs less to prevent poor indoor air quality than work through it or clean it up."

Like most occupational health issues, IAQ is highly politicized. In April of 1994, OSHA proposed an IAQ standard. It would have applied to 70 million workers in more than 4.5 million nonindustrial indoor work environments, including schools and training centers, offices, commercial establishments, health care facilities, cafeterias and factory break rooms.[2]

By the time the public comment period closed in August 1995, the agency had received 100,000 comments. Hearings ran from September 20, 1994 until March 13, 1995, with more than 400 witnesses testifying. Since then, however, the agency has been unable to issue a final indoor air quality standard. Although it remains on the long-term agenda, the timetable remains officially "undetermined."

In its 1999 long-term unified agenda, OSHA expressed continued intent to pass an IAQ standard. Describing the current situation, OSHA wrote:

"Thousands of heart disease deaths, hundreds of lung cancer deaths, and many cases of respiratory disease, Legionnaire's disease, asthma, and other ailments are estimated to be linked to this occupational hazard. EPA estimates that 20 to 35 percent of all workers in modern mechanically ventilated buildings may experience air-quality related signs and symptoms."[3]

Mike's latest indoor air quality investigation involves a newly renovated office contaminated with formaldehyde—a chemical slowly leaking out of glues, desks made of pressed woods, and other office materials. NIOSH describes the symptoms from formaldehyde as: eyes, nose, throat, respiratory system irritation; lacrimation (discharge of tears); cough; and bronchitis spasm. It also lists formaldehyde as a potential occupational carcinogen.

The NIOSH 8-hour recommended exposure limit for formaldehyde is 0.016 ppm while OSHA's limit is 0.75 ppm.[4] Although both these limits are low, the NIOSH limit is 47 times lower than the legally required OSHA limit. Mike laments, "The air sampling showed levels were less than the OSHA limit but approached the NIOSH limit. Of course, the

client wants to know what the results were and are they 'safe?'
How do I explain what is safe when the legal limit and the recommended limit are so far apart?"

Both limits are calculated for healthy adult workers, but in
this case, teens will also be exposed. Mike's client is a public
high school.

***

Poor air quality is not the only threat facing non-industrial
workers. Also crossing workplace boundaries are the hazards of
violence, bloodborne pathogens, vehicle accidents, and
ergonomics. While manufacturing and construction still bear
traditional risks, today's office workers, health care providers,
social service personnel, retail and service workers can also face
serious threats. Occupational hazards don't discriminate based
on location, pay or job title.

The blue and white-collar stereotypes that were accurate
when America supported itself with manufacturing are fading as
we continue living in the unprecedented information age.
Although traditional blue and white-collar jobs remain, there
are a lot less uniformed factory workers punching timecards. As
the income gap continues to grow, as manufacturing jobs ship
out of the country and as service industries expand in dramatic
numbers, there are fewer blue-collar jobs.

How less blue is America? In 1998, manufacturing account-
ed for just 13 percent of employment. By 2008, that number is
expected to decrease to 12 percent despite an overall growth of
14 percent in total employment over the same 10-year period.[5]
In other words, while manufacturing jobs are expected to
decline by 89,000, production is expected to remain constant or
even increase. While new technologies and automation may
ease some of the burden, in most cases, workers left in the factory will be expected to increase production and do more with
less. The remaining blue-collar workers will more aptly be
described as the black and blue workers.

In recent years, the line between white and blue collars has faded until it is no longer a line but a range, filled with its own new job type—light blue collar work. The increase in services plus the cost cutting trend of replacing professionals with assistants has resulted in the growth of light blue collar workers, such as physician's assistants, computer technicians, teacher's assistants, nurse's aides, and lab technicians. The Pharmacy Technician Certification Board, for example, certified more than 80,300 pharmacy technicians just since it began in 1995. Pharmacy technicians can fill and label prescriptions and generally assist the pharmacist "under direct supervision and in accordance with local, state, federal and Company regulations."[6]

Ergonomic hazards are the most widespread occupational hazard. They can be found in all sectors of the workforce, particularly in light blue-collar workplaces like hospitals. Nearly two million workers suffer work-related musculoskeletal disorders every year; 600,000 are so severe the workers lose time from work as a result. Some are permanently disabled. Almost fifteen percent of MSDs in private industry occurred in the health care sector to the same people working to make others well, usually from lifting and moving patients in hospitals and nursing homes.[7] Despite being the most costly and prevalent occupational hazard, OSHA has been unable to issue an ergonomics standard and may never overcome its hurdles. (See chapter 7 for more on ergonomics.)

Ironically, hospitals have become one of the most dangerous places to work. The situation was recently explained to the U.S. House of Representatives, Subcommittee on Workforce Protections by Bill Borwegen, Occupational Health and Safety Director for the Service Employees International Union (SEIU). Mr. Borwegen stated that healthcare workers are facing an epidemic of on-the-job injuries and illnesses. He said:

Healthcare workers have experienced a doubling of their workplace injury and illness rates over the past decade. Healthcare employers report that their workers suffered 652,800 injuries and illnesses in 1997, more than any other sector of the economy.

As startling as this may sound, today, it is safer to work in a factory, a mine, or on a construction site, than in a healthcare institution. In 1996, for the first time, the hospital worker injury and illness rate of 11.0 per 100 workers per year actually exceeded the rates for workers employed in these other industries that have traditionally been viewed as much more hazardous. Injury and illness rates for nursing home workers are far worse, reaching as high as 18.2 per 100 workers per year as recently as 1995. Yet the actual number of injuries and illnesses healthcare workers experience may in fact be at least double this figure, as it is estimated that less than 10% of the 600,000 to one million needlestick injuries healthcare workers suffer each year ever get reported in these statistics."[8]

According to the Bureau of Labor and Statistics, almost one of every two nonfarm wage and salary jobs added to the economy during the 1998-2008 period will be in health services, business services, social services, and engineering, management, and related services. Professional specialty occupations, computer engineers and medical assistants for example, will grow the fastest and add 5.3-million jobs. Service-producing industries will account for virtually all job growth with service workers expected to add 3.9 million jobs. Clearly, light blue-collar work is growing.

The 10 fastest growing occupations, 1998-2008[9]
[Numbers in thousands of jobs]

Occupation	Employment		Change	
	1998	2008	No.	%
Computer engineers	299	622	323	108
Computer support specialists	429	869	439	102
Systems analysts	617	1,194	577	94
Database administrators	87	155	67	77
Desktop publishing specialists	26	44	19	73
Paralegals and legal assistants	136	220	84	62
Persnl care & home health aides	746	1,179	433	58
Medical assistants	252	398	146	58
Social & human service assistants	268	410	141	53
Physician assistants	66	98	32	48

While their responsibilities are similar to white collar workers, light blue collar workers have less formal schooling than their professional counterparts. They also earn less money and receive fewer benefits. Their jobs, however, can be equally, if not more, dangerous. Since most light blue collar work does not appear overtly hazardous and because the workers have some level of technical knowledge, employers tend to assume they are safe. Instead, light blue collars tend to fall through the regulatory cracks to face hazards like physical strain, repetitive stress, workplace violence and bloodborne pathogens.

With massive retail chains like Wal-Mart sprawling all over the country, yet another type of worker category has emerged— the smocks. Retail sales, cashiers and clerk positions are three of the top 10 largest growth job categories.

Smocks wear the colors of restaurant chains, the emblems of hotels, or store names in big print on the back. Smocks are bright white behind pricey make-up counters, butter stained behind movie counters, greasy brown behind grills, or colorful and cheery, like those worn in hospitals. Smock jobs have high turnover, low training and low pay. They also tend to have high injury and illness rates.

Workplace violence has grabbed media attention in recent years with its unexpected and gruesome aftermath. News reports include disturbing footage of corporate environments barricaded with police tape and glimpses of sobbing, shocked families and co-workers. But rampage murders in offices are not the trend; the bigger story unfolds slowly, less dramatically.

According to the Department of Justice's National Crime Victimization Survey (NCVS), more retail sales workers are attacked each year than police officers, suffering 330,000 annual attacks compared with 234,000 police officers attacks. The NCVS estimates assaults and threats at work to number almost 2 million a year; of those, 396,000 are aggravated assaults, 51,000 are rapes, 84,000 are robberies and 1,000 are murders. Sales workers are the most murdered worker with annual averages near 327 from 1993 to 1996. In comparison, 74 taxi drivers and chauffeurs were murdered on the job.[10] OSHA has issued only voluntary guidelines on workplace violence, no regulations.

The general public isn't what it used to be. In the mixed-bag that is America, the world-economy of the 21st Century heralds a workforce of blue collar workers, white collar workers, light blue collar workers, and workers wearing smocks. In the palette of color, not even the remaining white collars are immune from the epidemic of workplace injuries and illnesses.

***

Changes in the modern workplace, workforce and economy have caused occupational hazards to change, spread and in many cases, multiply. Some are quiet and imperceptible, like poor indoor air quality, while others are hidden in the indifference born of familiarity, like the threat of ergonomic or chemical illness from having "always done it that way."

The old stereotype that blue-collar workers face all the health and safety risks is no longer true. Yes, we have traditional jobs with traditional hazards but today's workers can face jobsite dangers everywhere, not just in manufacturing or construction.

In his book, "The Working Class Majority: America's Best Kept Secret," author and economics professor Michael Zweig explains how the "working class" has disappeared with the current perception of the American population as lower, middle and upper class based on wealth and lifestyle. Instead, Professor Zweig suggests defining class by one's level of power. He says, "The majority of people are in the working class, those who do the direct work of production and who typically have little control over their jobs and no supervisory authority over others. The working class is the clear majority of the labor force, 62 percent. At the top of the class order, controlling the big business apparatus, is the capitalist class, about 2 percent of the labor force. A small fraction of the capitalist class operates on a national scale, and an even smaller network of several tens of thousands of interlocking directors among the largest of businesses is the core of the national ruling class. Between the capitalist class and the working class is the middle class, about 36 percent of the labor force."[11]

Zweig says, "Class is one of America's best kept secrets. Any serious discussion has been banished from polite conversation. But classes exist anyway, and the force of events is bringing class back into focus.[12] ....The sooner we realize that classes exist and understand the power relations that are driving the economic and political changes swirling around us, the sooner we will be able to build a new politics that engages people by wrestling with reality. The potential power of an openly working class politics is one of the most exciting and difficult issues of the new century."[13]

Therein lies hope for a cure for America's occupational illnesses and injuries. To date, the working class has largely relegated occupational health and safety to powerful employers and government officials. They have failed to represent the interests of the worker. In fact, politicians now go so far as to refer to labor as a "special interest." At 62% of the population, the working class is no special interest. Wearing blue collars, white collars, light-blue collars and smocks, it has more than enough weight to balance the scale against the capitalist class.

Says Zweig, "There can be no capitalism without a working class that constitutes the majority of the labor force. That's the structure of the game."[14]

CHAPTER 4

Our Current, Defunct
Surveillance System

Americans live in a world James Bond only dreamed about. Not long ago, the microwave and automatic garage door opener were luxury items. Today, high tech gadgets like laptop computers, cellular telephones, digital cameras and scanners are the norm. Bar codes and infrared pens zip us through airports, stores, and libraries; DNA testing sheds light on crimes, paternity, and disease traits; and Global Positioning Systems (GPS) use satellites to map everything from holes in the ozone layer to individual car locations. America's technology holds so much information that privacy advocates struggle just to keep up.

Still, we begin the 21st Century with no record, no master list or computer inventory in any public or private agency of work-related exposures, illnesses, injuries or even deaths. We have no such occupational health database because we have no accurate, comprehensive, national surveillance system.[1]

In September of 2000, NIOSH released its new "Worker Health Chartbook," a first of its kind compilation of occupational health and safety data into one reference. It begins by acknowledging an occupational health gap, stating: "Although our ability to monitor these outcomes has improved over time, this Chartbook illustrates the continued fragmentation of occupational health surveillance systems as well as the paucity (or even total absence) of data for certain occupational disorders and groups."[2]

Further on, NIOSH explains the problems:

Some of the reported values represent estimates based on statistical samples of populations, whereas others represent actual counts of cases. Some systems concentrate on workers only, and others report on all U.S. residents aged 15 and older. In addition, most data are restricted to private-sector workers. Public-sector workers (i.e. Federal, State and municipal workers) may be included in some data systems such as fatality surveys and case-based surveillance systems, but the coding may not permit exact numbers to be determined. Consequently, public workers, a large segment of the U.S. workforce, are not described accurately.[3]

Digging on through 250-pages of text, data and glossy colored charts, readers find the fatal illness section beginning bluntly with, "No surveillance data exist for most fatal occupational illnesses."[4] Among other overlooked, life-claiming illnesses are: work-related cancers; respiratory, circulatory, and central nervous system diseases; and kidney and liver disorders. The unknown occupational illness situation is a huge, insidious health problem buried in the middle of the NIOSH Chartbook where the public never finds it.

Even with its inaccuracies and omissions, the bottom line of the government's most current and comprehensive data source on occupational health and safety is that in 1997, workers were non-fatally injured or made ill at a rate ranging anywhere from a low of 4.4% in New York to a high of 10% in Wisconsin. The average national rate—an admittedly lowball estimate—was 7.1 cases per 100 full-time workers,[5] excluding fatalities and the even more common occupational illnesses.

If 7.1% of any other population was injured or made ill each year by anything other than the workplace, there would be a national outcry. Manufacturers would issue mass recalls of drugs, food and toys. The press would televise warnings and daytime talk shows would feature experts and true stories about the injured. Instead, the damaged population is workers and the response is silence.

In the summer of 2000, Firestone recalled 14.4 million tires after 285 crashes resulted in 123 fatalities. Just nine months later, Ford recalled 13 million more Firestone tires after eight crashes and 12 fatalities.[6] The ensuing national press coverage was enormous. Millions of dollars were spent. Congress held hearings on the matter and the Department of Transportation began a formal investigation "animated by a focused urgency, and a vigorous resolve to protect the public."[7] In contrast, no such response results from the hundreds of thousands of preventable worker injuries, illnesses, and deaths that occur each year.

Without adequate occupational health monitoring, we can't detect occupational disease and injury until so many occur that they become obvious. Imagine the same, crazy approach towards drinking water safety—water would be tested only when people get sick in numbers high enough to relate to water consumption in a certain area. Imagine restaurants being inspected after patrons report food-related illnesses; public schools holding fire drills after a fire; or medicines being tested after adverse reactions. No other public health issue in this country is treated as cavalierly as occupational health and safety.

There is a well-known management saying: "What gets counted counts." Another is "What gets measured gets managed." Referred to as benchmarking, both government and businesses use this standard management practice to direct activities and monitor progress.

In 1970, Congress literally wrote "what gets measured gets managed" into the OSHA Act by requiring occupational health and safety surveillance. The requirement was two-fold: 1) employers had to keep injury and illness records and 2) government had to collect and review those records. Together, these two components would provide Congress with the necessary information to manage the state of worker health and safety. The need for data was recognized then and now; it just has not been carried out.

Knowing where, how and when people become ill or injured helps target prevention efforts to make the most improvement. Equally important, data is a driving force behind funding. It justifies cost and documents results—both good and bad. Like a map, it shows where we have been and where we are headed. We have scant occupational health data. We are lost.

Counting, Estimating and Guessing

The recordkeeping section of the OSHA Act requires employers to "maintain accurate records of, and to make periodic reports on, work-related deaths, injuries and illnesses other than minor injuries requiring only first aid treatment and which do not involve medical treatment, loss of consciousness, restriction of work or motion, or transfer to another job."[8] This first half of the surveillance assignment—the recordkeeping part—went to OSHA. The second half—the data collection and analysis[9]—went to the Bureau of Labor Statistics (BLS). Neither did their job well.

OSHA's recordkeeping half of the surveillance scheme is critical. Without good records to draw from, there are no good statistics. Because OSHA's records exclude small employers, entire industries, government employees and the self-employed, they reflect only one-fifth of the American workplace. And even those numbers are questionable since they come from employers reporting on themselves and there are no systematic checks against medical or insurance records.

One big problem in the current system is that OSHA exempts more employers than it regulates. Another is excluding small employers; they have notoriously high injury rates. A third problem is excluding public employees, a huge disservice to the very people who make our government work. Workers in state hospitals, jails, and sewage treatment plants facing workplace violence, chemical exposure, confined spaces and blood-borne pathogens are among those ignored. A fourth troublesome exclusion is the exemption of supposedly low hazard industries, including retail trade, finance, insurance, and services like window cleaning or janitorial.[10] Of the 6.9 million establishments covered by OSHA and the State Plans, approximately 5.5 million are exempt because of their small size or type of business.[11]

OSHA injury and illness recordkeeping requirements are far from burdensome. First, there are no forms to fill out if an employer has no injuries or illnesses. Second, OSHA requires only that employers keep three completed forms in their files; employers are not required to report them unless OSHA specifically asks to see them during an audit or survey. Third, most insurance companies and responsible companies already require this type of information for their own internal accident prevention programs.

OSHA does require all employers to report fatalities or three hospitalizations (3 or more employees hospitalized within 30 days from the same incident) because the agency wants to learn about catastrophes, events like explosions, chemical spills, and structure failures. At the same time, employers can legally sustain daily injuries or illnesses and not report them to OSHA.

Employees at Tomaso Mulciber, Inc., for example, suffered over 60 crushed fingers—including finger amputations—before an OSHA inspection found more than two-thirds of the welding and assembly machines were unguarded. More than 600 employees work at this Columbus, Ohio plant making front end frames for Honda of America. At the time of the 1998 OSHA inspection, workers there faced an injury rate of 13.3 per 100 workers, nearly twice the average rate for auto manufacturers.[12]

Hospitals and doctors receiving injured or ill workers have no OSHA reporting obligations, and since employees make no separate report to OSHA when they become injured or ill, there is no system of checks and balances. Instead, the current system relies on employers to honestly report how many workers they injured, made ill or killed.

Published in the federal register, a 1997 suggestion to OSHA read, "The accuracy and usefulness of OSHA's reporting system would be vastly improved if it were to shift responsibility from employers (who have a vested interest in concealment) to the emergency rooms of hospitals and clinics. Hospitals are accustomed to reporting requirements, use the correct terminology in describing the accident and its subsequent treatment and are computerized."[13] Although implementing this one idea would vastly improve the entire surveillance system at little cost, it has not been done.[14]

***

Each year, the BLS conducts an annual survey of randomly selected establishments in private industry to collect data on occupational injury and illness. Perhaps the largest problem with the BLS survey is the sample size—165,000 establishments out of more than 6 million, or 2.8 percent. A 2.8 percent sample is not big enough. Worse, instead of growing with the workforce, the sample size shrunk in 1996 due to budget cuts, down from an already unimpressive 4.2 percent.[15]

OSHA and the BLS are aware of the system's inadequacies. So is Congress. In 1985, fifteen years after it wrote the OSHA Act, Congress requested an evaluation of both the available data and the data collection systems. Congress was told that there was so little agreement about the number of workplace-related illnesses that investigators would not take a position on the controversy about the "correct" number. The report concluded, "Most death and injuries occur one at a time or in small numbers in the nation's more than 4.5 million workplaces."[16] (The number of workplaces has since grown to 6 million.)

Since that report and in response to a 1987 study confirming the problem, the BLS improved the annual survey to collect

more information on injured workers and incident circumstances.[17] Along with expanding the annual survey in the early
1990's, the BLS started the Census of Fatal Occupational
Injuries (CFOI). While not perfect, CFOI is the most thorough
and accurate collection of fatality data to date since it gathers
information from diverse sources including death certificates,
state workers' compensation reports, news media, and motor
vehicle incident reports. But CFOI collects data only on deaths
from injuries, not deaths from illnesses which occur in far
greater numbers. Even with CFOI, we still don't have the true
occupational illness picture.

The BLS does not hide its illness omission. Underreporting
is explained in the main BLS rulebook—the *BLS Handbook of
Methods*.[18] It's also explained in the annual Workplace Injury
and Illness Summary press releases. For example, in the 2000
press release, the agency admits:

"The survey measures the number of new work-related illness cases that are recognized, diagnosed, and reported during
the year. Some conditions (for example, long-term latent illnesses caused by exposure to carcinogens) often are difficult to
relate to the workplace and are not adequately recognized and
reported. These long-term latent illnesses are believed to be
understated in the survey's illness measures. In contrast, the
overwhelming majority of the reported new illnesses are those
that are easier to directly relate to workplace activity (for example, contact dermatitis or carpal tunnel syndrome)."[19]

In fact, the BLS found that of the 5.7 million injuries and illnesses reported in private industry in 1999, 93.5% were injuries.
Only 372,000 cases were illnesses. Of those, 66% were noise
induced hearing loss and ergonomic ailments like carpal tunnel
syndrome. Clearly, illnesses like cancer, chemical sensitivity,
and reproductive disorders are not being reported, therefore,
they are not compiled into the BLS statistics.

The chronic failure to count and measure work-related

exposures, injuries and illnesses—the lack of surveillance—dramatically illustrates the unimportance of worker health and welfare. This is especially so since the governing agencies and Congress clearly realize how critical a management tool it is. Indeed, the frank admission and acceptance of missed illness data by Congress, OSHA, NIOSH and BLS is not only against the letter of the OSHA law, it defies the moral intent behind the law to provide workplaces free from recognizable hazards. Because the problem has been known for so long by the government agencies tasked with controlling it proves that they have accepted it.

There is no doubt that it is difficult to identify all occupational diseases and link them to specific workplaces. Among the confounding factors: diseases can have long latency periods; people switch jobs and relocate; and exposures occur off the job that may influence disease promotion or progression. Just because illness data collection is tricky, however, does not warrant ignoring it. Manageable hindrances left unaddressed for more than 30 years are not hindrances, they are excuses.

Congress does not excuse the Internal Revenue Service from catching tax evaders because there are complicated ways to cheat. The Federal Bureau of Investigation is not relieved of its responsibility to thwart terrorism and hate crimes because the Internet has made them easier. And ultimately, the nation did not throw its collective hands in the air in defeat when the seemingly unbeatable AIDS virus began to take its deadly bite. What was required, however, was public awareness and pressure to do the right thing. Workplace health and safety will require the same. Apparently, if the public is not outraged, Congress won't be.

Misleading Headlines

BLS is not mandated to implement the OSHA Act; that is OSHA's job. BLS's job is to measure labor statistics, and admittedly, the numbers are not there to easily count. Still, BLS is shrugging its shoulders and letting the need go unmet rather than decry the problem or adjust its numbers to accommodate underestimates.

The BLS, for example, takes a confident stance when releasing injury and illness statistics. The agency reported in 1999:

"A total of 5.7 million injuries and illnesses were reported in private industry workplaces during 1999, resulting in a rate of 6.3 cases per 100 equivalent full-time workers, according to a survey by the Bureau of Labor Statistics, U.S. Department of Labor. Employers reported a 4 percent drop in the number of cases and a 2 percent increase in the hours worked compared with 1998, reducing the case rate from 6.7 in 1998 to 6.3 in 1999. The rate for 1999 was the lowest since the Bureau began reporting this information in the early 1970s."[20]

While the BLS isn't lying in its opening statement, the overlooked catch phrase is "were reported." Unfortunately, most users of this data don't realize that occupational illnesses are so severely under-reported and that all rates are skewed.

A similar message was provided by Alexis Herman, Secretary of Labor (the BLS's boss) on the same day.

> Workplace injury and illness rates declined in 1999 for the seventh straight year–nearly a 30 percent drop since 1992. This steady trend downward shows that employers and workers are making occupational safety and health a high priority. That's good news for business, workers and all Americans.
>
> Injuries and illnesses dropped 4 percent in 1999 even though employment rose 2 percent. That means 200,000 more workers went home to their families without a job-related injury or illness than in 1998.
>
> I am delighted with the progress we have made together with workers and employers in job safety and health during the Clinton Administration. We said we would measure our success by whether injuries and illnesses declined. They have–continuously and signifi-

cantly. These efforts must continue until every worker
goes home whole and healthy every day.[21]

That is the entire text of the Secretary's statement; there are
no explanations of data limitations. "Delight" and back-patting
might be deserved if the BLS's survey rates could be confident-
ly relied on to represent the national picture. They can't. The
truth is that even though the BLS's survey rates may be going
down, those rates don't represent the national workplace.
Downplaying the large, well documented problems with occupational health and safety surveillance is one of the reasons why
the epidemic of work-related injuries and illnesses remains
unknown. It is also one of the reasons it continues.

Businesses, the media and the professional health and safety
community all mimic the confident message from the BLS,
trickling down only the alleged conclusions. Some examples of
the news reports based on BLS's faulty data:

"Workplace injuries killed 6,023 Americans last year, 32
fewer than in 1998 despite an increase in employment, the
Labor Department reported."[22] Wall Street Journal (front page).

"The rate of occupational injuries and illnesses declined for
the fifth straight year in 1997, the Bureau of Labor Statistics
reported Thursday. Labor Secretary Alexis Herman called the
numbers "good news to our nation's work force."[23] The Augusta
Chronicle, December 1998.

"The overall rates of U.S. worker illnesses and injuries have
fallen dramatically since 1993, according to the Bureau of Labor
Statistics." American Industrial Hygiene Association, 2000
Fact Sheet on Occupational and Environmental Health and
Safety Week.

"The good news is that injury and illness rates are down by
22 percent since President Clinton took office. Fatalities on the
job have declined to an all-time low."[24] Charles Jeffress, head of
OSHA, in a May, 2000 speech to the American Industrial
Hygiene Conference and Exposition.

Press releases are written to deliver short, concise information. The press grabs a few sentences, makes it a headline, and prints it. OSHA, industry, and the rest of the safety and health community[25] do the same. This is why the BLS needs to dramatically change its tune.

Taking its lead from the BLS wording, the media passes along a skewed impression to the public. Without accurate press coverage of true workplace conditions, there does not appear to be anything to be concerned about. Most people, therefore, are unconcerned about workplace health because they don't see the problem, not because they don't care. Meanwhile, Congress continues to mismanage what it mis-measures.

***

BLS numbers are not the only estimates available on workplace injuries and illnesses. On July 28, 1997, an independent team of experts—J. Paul Leigh, Steven Markowitz, Marianne Fahs, Chonggak Shin and Philip Landrigan—published a study in the prestigious, peer-reviewed Archives of Internal Medicine. Supported by NIOSH and the Economic Policy Institute, the team concluded, " Approximately 6,500 job-related deaths from injury, 13.2 million nonfatal injuries, 60,300 deaths from disease, and 862,200 illnesses are estimated to occur annually in the civilian American workforce."[26]

Part of that same team, J. Paul Leigh, Steven Markowitz, Marianne Fahs, and Philip Landrigan, expanded the original 1997 study into the book, "Costs of Occupational Injuries and Illnesses." They concluded, "Whereas reported cases of injuries appear to be slowly increasing over time, reported cases of diseases and conditions are rising rapidly."[27] This is a very different picture than that presented by BLS and forwarded to the public.

Leigh et al. found the BLS survey undercounted *injuries* by roughly 53% due to the exemptions of public employers, the self-employed and intentional underreporting by the surveyed employers. When the BLS was asked if it would adjust its numbers to accommodate these types of estimated undercounts, the agency said no, because it only measures specific activities and does not make projections.[28]

The BLS should, therefore, begin its annual press release on occupational health by saying something like, "Although we measure only about 3% of the private sector; and we exclude public employers even though they operate dangerous environments like landfills, sewage treatment plants and hospitals; and we only survey companies in certain industries with 10 or more employees; and we exclude part-timers even though it is a hazardous and growing workforce; and we know that we miss most data on illnesses like cancer or birth defects related to work; well, we think there were about 5.7 million injuries and illnesses but we could be way off because occupational illness is a real wild card. Still, we found 6.3 cases per 100 full time workers."

Quiet Cronies

Major safety and health professional associations produce standards, guidelines, training and priorities based largely on BLS survey data. Senior leaders from these groups comment to Congress on major safety and health legislation. While they can't be expected to repeat data limitations every time, and while they should be able to quickly tap into accurate surveillance data, they can't because it doesn't exist. In the meanwhile, they need to stop pretending that it does. Failing to acknowledge the problem is making it worse.

Instead of educating the public about the shocking illness estimates and the uncertainty of the issue, the professional community and the government have looked the other way. This is a massive failure by OSHA, NIOSH, BLS, and the major health and safety organizations like the National Safety Council, the American Industrial Hygiene Association and the American Society of Safety Engineers—organizations supposedly committed to improving worker health and safety. Their silence in response to this problem, especially after the Leigh team's study and book, speak volumes about the missions of these organizations. None have chosen to aggressively advocate for better illness data.[29]

The OSHA Act requires employers to comply with OSHA standards and make workplaces free from "recognizable hazards that are causing or are likely to cause death or serious physical harm to his employees." The word "recognizable" makes reasonable the expectations placed on employers.

Employers are not mind readers able to see into the future and somehow predict what might later be found hazardous. Realizing this, Congress wrote into the OSHA Act that employers would be required to control only **recognized** hazards **provided that** surveillance be performed to recognize new and emerging hazards. The clear intent was to place realistic expectations on employers, NOT to provide a loophole for dismissing potential hazards because they may be difficult—troublesome even—to record and monitor.

The OSHA Act was created "...to assure so far as possible every working man and woman in the Nation safe and healthful working conditions and to preserve our human resources..." It does not add "unless it is too cumbersome in which case you are excused from making the effort..." Who decided that the difficulty in tracking the injuries and illnesses was more onerous than suffering them?

***

The Workplace—A Big Piece of the Environmental Puzzle

Ebola virus, mad cow disease, flesh eating bacteria, and antibiotic resistance are modern public health issues right out of a science fiction movie. Likewise, a story about the world's wealthiest nation polluting itself into illness and death sounds like a children's fable warning against recklessness and greed. It may be true.

According to Lowell Weicker Jr., Chairman of the Pew Environmental Health Commission, "We responded quickly to the threat of West Nile virus, tracking and monitoring every report of infected birds and people, but 20 years into the asthma epidemic, this country is still unable to track where and when attacks occur and what environmental links may trigger them."[30]

The Pew Environmental Health Commission, supported by the nonprofit Pew Charitable Trusts, warns, "We have as a nation invested heavily in identifying and tracking pollutants in the environment, particularly for regulatory and ecological purposes, but only minimally in tracking exposures and the distribution of disease and its relationship to the environment. As a result of decades of neglect, we have a public health system that is working without even the most basic information about chronic disease and potential environmental factors."[31] They offer the following proof:

- Only four states track autoimmune diseases like Lupus even though rates are believed to be rising;

- While learning disabilities rose 50 percent in the past 10 years, only six states track the disorders;

- Most states do not track severe developmental disabilities like autism, cerebral palsy and mental retardation nor do they track endocrine or metabolic disorders and neurological conditions like multiple sclerosis (despite evidence showing that rates are increasing);

- There is no systemic tracking for most U.S asthma cases (they increased 75 percent between 1980 and 1994) and,

- Less than half of the nation has birth defect registries even though birth defects are the leading cause of infant death.[32]

In September of 2000, the Pew Environmental Health Commission released its major report, "America's

Environmental Health Gap: Why the Country Needs a Nationwide Health Tracking Network." It said, "The federal government tracks many things all the time. It knows how many women dye their hair every year (three out of five), but has only rough estimates of how many people have Parkinson's disease, asthma, or most other chronic diseases that cause four of every five deaths in the U.S. each year. We have a right to know more."[33]

The report explained how most people are unaware of the lack of health surveillance. It stated, "Recent public opinion research confirms that Americans want to have access to national, state and community level health data. In fact, they are incredulous when informed that health tracking information is not readily available."[34]

Just a few months before the Pew Environmental Health Commission report and at the request of nine members of Congress, the U.S. General Accounting Office (GAO) did a study of the nation's data on human exposure to potentially toxic chemicals. The GAO similarly concluded, "The nation has a long way to go in measuring human exposure to potentially harmful chemicals."[35]

While environmental health monitoring is desperately needed and long overdue, occupational health surveillance is arguably the most critical missing piece of the puzzle. The workplace is the mother lode of all environmental contaminants and exposures, possibly the nation's greatest source of nonhereditary disease. Most of what leaches into our drinking water, contaminates our food and pollutes our air comes from workplaces, where it first damages workers. Monitoring environmental health effects without including occupational health is like treating symptoms without diagnosing the disease. It is reactive. It makes no sense.

***

Case in Point—Libby, MT

Vermiculite is the white airy material added to potting soil to improve drainage. Asbestos is a naturally occurring mineral fiber that causes lung cancer, asbestosis and mesothelioma, a quick-killing cancer of the lining of the lung. In the small town of Libby, Montana, both co-existed peacefully underground. Then they were dug up.

For 60 years, vermiculite was mined in Libby for insulation, lawn and garden products, and construction materials. W.R. Grace and Co. (the same company featured in the bestseller and hit movie, A Civil Action) owned and operated the mine from 1963 until 1990 where it generated nearly 80 percent of the world's vermiculite.

Asbestos was so poorly managed at the mine that when the EPA received dusty file boxes from W.R. Grace and Co., they tested them for asbestos. The samples were positive and the half-dozen boxes had to be quarantined.[36]

Now, a full scale EPA surveillance program is in place to determine the health impact from Libby's uncontrolled exposure to asbestos. A massive site cleanup is also underway. Roughly 6,200 Libby residents and former residents will receive federal medical screens including a chest x-ray and lung function test.[37]

The asbestos exposure trail extends far beyond the 200 deaths and the 900 or so expected cases of lung disease linked to the mine.[38] Ore from the W.R. Grace vermiculite mine went to 300 locations where more workers, their families, and their communities could have been exposed. Consumers face exposure to asbestos in, among other things, lawn and garden products containing vermiculite.[39] The W.R. Grace and Co. product manufactured with the asbestos-containing vermiculite is insulation named Zonolite. Zonolite is still in homes, schools and businesses everywhere.

Mines are regulated under the Mine Safety and Health Act

(MSHA) instead of OSHA. For workers in general industry and construction, the OSHA PEL for asbestos is 0.1 asbestos fibers per cubic centimeter of air.[40] For mines, the MSHA PEL is twenty times that high at 2 fibers per centimeter of air[41] even though the lungs of miners are no hardier than those in private industry, their lives no less valuable.

MSHA tried to lower the asbestos PEL in 1989 to OSHA's lower level of 0.1 fiber. The Seattle Post-Intelligencer (the paper that broke the Libby asbestos story, calling it *An Uncivil Action*) described what happened next this way:

"As it does every time the government proposes to reduce exposure to any asbestos fiber, the industry flooded MSHA with opposition to the agency's proposal."[42] Among the opposition was W.R Grace and the Asbestos Information Association, an industry-funded lobbying group claiming that the risk of asbestos exposure from the mines was minimal.

Now, the government is spending millions of taxpayer dollars while 6,200 Montanans wait a stressful three months to learn the results of their medical tests. And since a ban on asbestos in consumer products was lifted in 1991, asbestos-contaminated vermiculite products will continue to migrate into consumer hands after being handled by unknown numbers of workers.

If the owners of the vermiculite mine in Libby ran it safely for the workers, the town would also have been protected. The workers and their families in the 300 or so locations that processed the product after it left the mine would also have been safe. Consumers would not unwittingly handle asbestos contaminated materials and the public, like the Libby families living between Zonolite insulated walls, would not wonder if their homes will make their children ill.

Since the mine did not adequately control asbestos exposure on its own, occupational heath surveillance could have served as a second-tier safety net. It could have prevented the Libby health nightmare by detecting asbestos-related disease before hundreds of people succumbed. Now, nothing can help the people—both the public and the workers—destined to slowly choke to death from a preventable asbestos-related lung disease.

***

Prevention—the Flip Side of the Surveillance Coin

Surveillance is to occupational health what diagnosis is to medicine. It is like a blood test. It is our diagnosis, indicating where our problems are. Without it, we don't know what to treat, let alone prevent.

Even if the current occupational surveillance system was perfect—and clearly it is not—it accepts a certain number of injuries, illnesses and deaths. Its accepts that a number of injuries, illnesses and deaths will occur before a hazard is recognized. How many is that? Who will suffer them?

Measurement does not have to occur after the fact; steps can and should be taken before harm occurs. The FAA does not wait until planes crash to investigate problems; instead, it responds to near misses recognizing that they very well could have been a crash. A sensitive reporting and response system of air traffic incidents benefits us all. No one would fly without it.

Even if the FAA were to callously and irresponsibly wait until planes actually crashed, at least the crashes would be noticed. For the estimated 60,300 people that slip into death each year from occupational disease, there is no crash. There are no flames, no news footage of charred wreckage, floating luggage, or bodies draped in white cloths. Nevertheless, 60,300 casualties result each year from occupational disease and roughly 6,000 deaths from traumatic injury. And their families grieve.

Surveillance is hindsight; it looks backwards at death, illness and suffering. Surveillance is not the solution, prevention is. If we monitor and clean up our nation's workplaces, we can prevent both occupational illness and environmental damage. Not only is it the right thing to do, it is easier and costs less.

Environmental problems are widespread, ill-defined, litigious, and expensive. But in the workplace, the population is identified; the chemicals are known; and the responsible party is the employer. If medical tests or treatment are needed, those affected are limited to the size of the workforce, not entire communities. Cleaning contaminated air in the workplace, for example, is easier and cheaper with local exhaust ventilation and air scrubbers versus the alternative of environmental air pollution, worker and community lung disease, accelerated building damage, and worldwide problems like global warming and holes in the ozone layer. Finally, it is not the taxpayer's job to clean up after businesses. Taxpayers paying to monitor and clean the environment are the same workers exposed on the job and polluted off the job.

Even with good occupational surveillance, monitoring the environment will always be necessary to confirm compliance and because Americans create environmental hazards un-related to work. We generate, landfill and incinerate mountains of trash; in most places, we drive cars instead of using mass transit systems; we consume electricity made from coal burning and nuclear power plants; we farm with fertilizers, pesticides, rodenticides and insecticides; and we eat beef and drink milk from cows injected with steroids, anti-biotics, and bovine-growth-hormone. Genetically modified foods are in our markets and persistent toxins like polychlorinated biphenyls (PCB's) are well lodged in our waterways.

PCB's climb the food-chain from the muck of river-bottom beds, into the fish we eat, and eventually settle into long-term storage in our fatty tissue cells. Nursing mothers dislodge those PCB's from breast tissue where they travel via breast milk into newborns. Long before those PCB's reached a riverbed, however, employers created them in refineries; loaded them into trucks, put them in electrical transformers, and released them in sufficient quantities to create an environmental hazard. Workers were exposed to PBC's long before the environment and innocent newborns. If we finally begin to adequately survey the workplace, we can protect workers as well as the environment and newborns.

Surveillance is the ultimate guard against both occupational and environmental pollution because it allows us to aim precisely at the point of exposure. This saves workers their health and protects unsuspecting communities from illnesses. It also guards employers running their companies in an ethical manner from the unfair advantage gained by those companies that cheat. Taxpayers save money by shifting the financial burden back to the source of the problem, the originator of the pollution. Lastly, the threat of surveillance will persuade some companies tempted by short-term profits to instead invest in the long-term health of their communities and workers.

It is time to invest in prevention by first investing in surveillance.

CHAPTER 5

Toxic Politics and Negotiable Exposures

Dispersed Wreckage

Michelle has a lung problem called sarcoidosis. A non-smoker, she has 60% of her lung capacity left.

Sarcoidosis is defined by the Mosby Medical Encyclopedia as: "a long-term disease of unknown origin marked by small, round bumps in the tissue around the organs of the body, usually the lungs, spleen, liver, skin, mucous membranes, and tear and salivary glands, usually along with the lymph glands. The sores usually go away after a period of some months or years, but lead to widespread grainy swelling and fibrosis."[1]

Michelle made computer chips using a caustic chemical named photoresist and two solvents, xylene and electronic grade acetone. She also was exposed to silicone and metals, including beryllium. One chemical Michelle worked bore the warning, "Lung Irritant" and "Carcinogen."

Although her company provided chemical training, performed air monitoring, and had ventilation, Michelle is still sick. Three years away from her pension, she says she doesn't mind using inhalers but begins to cry as she explains, "I could live a half-decent life using inhalers but the thought of dragging around an oxygen tank..."

Michelle may simply be the unfortunate victim of sarcoidosis, a disease of unknown origin. Or, she may be suffering from a lung condition caused by years of exposure to chemicals known to irritate the lungs. It could be from beryllium. Right now, no one knows.

Michelle was never personally monitored for exposure and

she has no exposure records of exactly what she breathed. She says, "They did have ventilation but then why did they pull pregnant women out of there so fast? You couldn't work in there even if you were trying to get pregnant."

Her primary care physician told her honestly that his diagnosis of sarcoidosis was essentially his best professional guess. Michelle has since seen a specialist at a major teaching hospital who, she says, "wants to perform a lung wash to get some tissues from my lungs and look at them to see exactly what they are doing and why."

As she speaks, Michelle pauses often for breath and wheezes a bit. Her voice is low and raspy. Her lungs lack the ability to power her voice normally; you can almost hear the 40% loss of lung function.

Since her workers compensation claim has been steadfastly refused, Michelle returned to work and struggles. She coughs, has difficulty breathing and feels generally lousy from the steroid medication she takes.

Michelle has no proof that she was over-exposed to anything. Of course, she has no proof that she wasn't either. She retained a lawyer and, in a few weeks, will travel two hours to the closest major city to have the lung wash. She will pay for it herself if her regular health insurance refuses to pay—it may since she filed for workers' compensation.

This is the frustrating legacy of poor surveillance and under-regulated chemical exposure. Employers have little incentive to perform adequate exposure monitoring. Employees generally are unaware of exactly what they breath or absorb and how much. Occupational illnesses are poorly recognized by the medical community; therefore, they are often treated incorrectly. Since most occupational illnesses go unrecognized, they go unreported; therefore, we do not detect or prevent them. As a result of all this, employers are not financially held accountable and they have little incentive to improve. In fact, many may not know they are harming their workers. Some don't want to know. In the end, it is individual employees like Michelle that quietly pay the price with their health and personal savings.

***

The Dose Makes the Poison

A favorite test question of industrial hygiene professors is "Who said 'The dose makes the poison'?" The answer is Paracelsus, back in the early 1500's, and his once-radical concept is what all our exposure limits are built on today.

Paracelsus explained his theory saying, "All substances are poisons; there is none which is not a poison. The right dose differentiates a poison and a remedy."[2] In other words, a specific amount of chemical over a certain time will cause an expected health effect. Conversely, there are doses which will not cause certain health effects. This is called the dose-response relationship. Essential to understanding which dose is remedy and which is poison, Paracelsus said, is scientific study.[3]

OSHA's chemical exposure limits are based on the assumption that there is a dose between zero and some scientifically determined number where no significant harm will occur—a so-called safe zone. OSHA calls these Permissible Exposure Limits (PELs), and they represent the upper boundary beyond which employers can not legally expose employees.[4]

OSHA is not the only agency publishing exposure limits. NIOSH, an independent research branch under the Centers for Disease Control, recommends exposure limits for 667 hazardous substances—about twice as many as OSHA. The American Conference of Governmental Industrial Hygienists (ACGIH) publishes hundreds of exposure limits each year, most more protective than OSHA's. The only legally enforceable exposure limits, however, are OSHA's. While some conscientious employers voluntarily comply with the more stringent, voluntary limits, many do not. Some don't realize OSHA's limits are inadequate, some don't know about the other recommended limits, and some don't comply with them because they don't have to.

An estimated 32 million U.S. workers are exposed to 650,000 hazardous chemicals in over 3 million American workplaces.[5] Every day, millions of workers use substances that have never been tested or have been incompletely tested. In other words, we don't understand the dose-response relationship. OSHA can not keep up with the flow of chemical exposure; the agency has established PELs for only about 300 chemicals, and most are grossly outdated. The nation lacks adequate health surveillance. This makes the modern workplace one big, unethical, uncontrolled and unproductive exposure experiment—and it is killing people.

**

Methylene Chloride: Just One Chemical

Each year, OSHA investigates worker fatalities from overexposure to Methylene Chloride (MC). Depending on the dose, MC exposure causes health effects ranging from eye, skin, and respiratory irritation to central nervous system impairments, heart and liver effects, cancer, coma and death.[6] One of the most widely used of all organic solvents, over a quarter of a million workers handle MC on the job—a population equal to that of many small cities, like that of Raleigh, North Carolina.

Most MC exposure occurs while stripping paint and furniture or cleaning metal. Workers also face MC exposure during manufacturing and when using MC-containing products such as paint, polyurethane foam, plastics, chemicals, adhesives and pharmaceuticals.[7] MC use occurs at approximately 91,600 U.S. workplaces - three times the number of McDonald's Restaurants in the entire world.[8]

PELs for gases are described in units called "parts per million" or ppm. Said another way, ppm is an amount of pollutant compared to an amount of air, specifically, one million parts of air. If air molecules were golf balls, 100 ppm would be 100 red golf balls in a pool of 1 million. 10,000 ppm means 1% of all the golf balls are red. While PELs often appear low, the red golf balls add up as billions of air molecules pass through the lungs each day. Over a week, a year and a working lifetime, the number of red golf balls can become enormous.

OSHA adopted its original MC PEL of 500 ppm in 1971 from a 1969 recommendation by the American National Standards Institute (ANSI).[9] An early warning about the inadequacy of the original PEL came only four years later when the ACGIH dramatically reduced their recommended exposure limit from 500 to 100 ppm.[10] A second warning came in 1976 when NIOSH recommended that OSHA reduce the MC PEL from 500 ppm to 75 ppm.[11] Despite these significant reductions recommended by two well-respected, independent organizations only 4 and 5 years later, the OSHA PEL stayed put until 1997. For 26 years, workers were exposed to MC based on science from the 1950's and 1960's instead of current information.

ACGIH and NIOSH were not the only scientific organizations recognizing the ill effects of MC and recommending lower exposure. In May of 1985, the Environmental Protection Agency (EPA) announced that MC was a probable human carcinogen.[12] In December of 1985, the U.S. Food and Drug Administration (FDA) published a proposal to ban the use of MC as an ingredient in aerosol cosmetic products. Just three years later, the FDA banned the use of MC in cosmetic products,[13] and the ACGIH again reduced its recommended exposure limit by cutting it in half.[14] In 1986, the U.S. Consumer Product Safety Commission proposed labeling household products as hazardous substances if users might breath MC.[15] Still, OSHA's MC PEL did not budge.

Also in the mid-1980's, the International Union, United Automobile, Aerospace and Agricultural Implement Workers of America (UAW) petitioned OSHA to quickly reduce workers' exposure to MC. The UAW requested that OSHA: (1) publish a hazard alert; (2) issue an emergency temporary standard; and (3) begin work on a new permanent standard for controlling MC exposure. Six more unions joined the UAW's petition. OSHA denied it, agreeing only to start work on a new permanent standard.

OSHA knew of the harmful and fatal effects of MC. In 1986, NIOSH recommended treating MC as a "potential occupational carcinogen" and reducing exposures to the lowest feasible limit.[16] At the time, there were 1 million workers handling MC.[17] Seven months later, OSHA announced that it was considering revising the exposure limit.[18] In 1988, ACGIH reduced its recommended MC exposure yet again. Still, it would take OSHA nine more years to take action.

When OSHA finally lowered the MC PEL in 1997, it estimated that the lower exposure limit would *annually* save an average of 31 lives from cancer, save 3 lives from acute central nervous system and oxygen deprivation, and prevent as many as 30,000 to 54,000 episodes of central nervous system effects and oxygen deprivation.[19] The U.S. demand for MC at the time was an unimaginable 285 *million* pounds.[20]

OSHA acknowledges that even at the reduced MC PEL of 25 ppm, the limit in effect today, the risks to workers remain clearly significant. In fact, if the 237,000 employees still using MC at their workplace are exposed to 25 ppm for their working lifetime, 8533 excess cancer deaths will still occur at the lower rate of 3.6 per 1,000 workers.

Because of the lack of documented *feasibility* data, OSHA has concluded that there is not enough information available to support lowering the MC PEL below 25 ppm. So, OSHA continues to gather information on the risks of MC exposure and the feasibility of compliance with a lower PEL to determine whether future rulemaking is appropriate. Meanwhile, today's

MC workers still face an excess lifetime cancer risk of 3.6 can-cers per 1000 workers as well as other, less studied ailments. Scarier still, for all those years that the PEL remained unneces-sarily high, workers carried an occupational lifetime estimated risk of 126 excess cancers per 1000 workers.[21]

MC has other effects besides cancer. Once in the body, MC breaks down into carbon monoxide—a well-known reproduc-tive hazard. Carbon monoxide damages the central nervous sys-tems of developing fetuses and slows fetal growth. Even though OSHA is concerned about this, the agency reduced the PEL to prevent cancer, not to prevent harm to developing fetuses. In the preamble to the long-awaited MC revision, OSHA confess-es that it is "sufficiently concerned about the potential for reproductive health effects of carbon monoxide as a result of MC metabolism that it has decided to continue to gather infor-mation and revisit this issue, if warranted."[22] On OSHA's clock, that could mean decades of unacceptable, dangerous exposure to developing fetuses.

***

Modern Chemical Exposure
and OSHA's 1989 PEL Update Attempt

MC is not an isolated case; it represents the norm for most of OSHA's chemical exposure limits. In more than 25 years, OSHA has managed to promulgate new PELs for only about two dozen substances.

OSHA does not hide its PEL problem. In several documents, including fact sheets and others posted on the internet, OSHA frankly admits that many of its PELs are inadequate.[23]

In 1989, OSHA attempted to address the PEL problem by basically revising its entire list of PELs for general industry. At that time, the agency estimated that the new limits would pro-vide additional health protection for over 21 million employees and eliminate 55,000 occupational illnesses and 683 deaths each year. OSHA further estimated that the new PEL list would have an annual cost of a fraction of 1% of the sales for the affected industry sectors.[24]

The AFL-CIO believed OSHA's new PEL standard should have included more monitoring and medical provisions and found a handful of the updated limits still too high. So, the AFL-CIO sued OSHA over the PEL update. Industry groups also sued, claiming that the new levels were too stringent and the regulatory process had been thwarted. Industry won. Three years later the 11th Circuit Court of Appeals rejected the adopted limits and OSHA was forced to enforce the old list of PELs—PELS based on the science of the 1950's and 1960's. Not much has happened since that 1989 court decision.

Updating PELs is no common sense process. Although many chemicals are similar in structure and toxicity, OSHA must individually assess each substance and document the scientific rationale for how it determined the level at which "material impairment" will occur. Furthermore, the agency must demonstrate economic and technological feasibility for each individual industry affected.[25] OSHA also has to hold public hearings and respond to both written and verbal comments. This is all in addition to actually researching and writing a new standard.

At the same time OSHA is jumping through it's legislative rulemaking hoops, it must simultaneously battle industry lobbyists, Congress and even unions. The process is expensive, political, time consuming, and impractical. It does not work, and because of it, people are exposed to limits known to be dangerous.

If it took 26 years for OSHA to address such a well-known and widely used chemical as MC, it is clearly impossible for OSHA to ever successfully update and expand the PEL list under its current restrictive system. So, while ACGIH and NIOSH can routinely update their lists of recommended exposure limits, OSHA's remain rooted in 50-year old science.

***

When Truth is Stranger Than Fiction

Ironically, OSHA is most often portrayed as an organization run amok with over-regulation. Despite this characterization, OSHA standards are not created in a vacuum by zealous safety and health advocates completely ignorant of the realities of the workplace.

According to the OSHA Act, OSHA must address toxic materials by setting standards "which most adequately assures, to the extent feasible, on the basis of the best available evidence, that no employee will suffer material impairment of health or functional capacity even if such employee has regular exposure to the hazard dealt with by such standard for the period of his working life."[26] OSHA must show that its health requirements are both technologically and economically feasible, conduct detailed economic analyses, and when data permits, perform quantitative risk assessments and then use those assessments to finally set exposure limits.

The ACGIH, NIOSH, and in many ways the EPA, are unencumbered by such requirements; instead, worker health is the bottom line. OSHA, on the other hand, can't adopt any recommendations, even NIOSH's, without first going through its lengthy rulemaking process. So, OSHA is left with outdated and incomplete standards, such as the antiquated PELs.

Just one of the requirements OSHA must meet when passing regulations is making them "technologically feasible." In its data collection efforts to update the hexavalent chromium standard, for example, OSHA explained this particular regulatory step in the 1996 Federal Register.

"To support its technological feasibility conclusions, OSHA must gather information on technological solutions for controlling hexavalent chromium exposure, including information on engineering controls, chemical substitution, process modifications, work practice controls, and personal protection equipment. OSHA particularly needs information linking data on the exposure control measures in use at the time of sampling and the levels of worker exposure to hexavalent chromium achieved with these controls in a wide variety of industries and job categories within these industries. Information of this type is essential in order to determine the technological feasibility of alternative PELs and to estimate the associated costs of compliance. The Agency proposes to conduct as many as 50 site visits to affected employers and to contact and interview by phone as many as 150 firms, trade associations, labor organizations, or experts."[27]

The cost of just this preliminary data collection effort for this one chemical was an estimated $341,250. (OSHA has still not managed to update the hexavalent chromium standard despite NIOSH recommending 100-fold reductions as far back as 1975.)

In addition to determining if a new standard is technologically feasible, OSHA must perform an economic analysis to determine how much it will cost. The Regulatory Flexibility Act requires that OSHA measure the potential economic impact to determine whether proposed standards may have significant impact on a substantial number of small entities. Public hearings are held. As a result of this open process, the final MC standard contained delayed implementation dates, reduced paperwork requirements, streamlined medical surveillance provisions and other accommodations that would minimize costs for small employers help them to meet the standard's protective goals.[28] In the case of the lead standard, OSHA granted 10 years for the primary lead industry to build in the engineering controls needed to reduce exposure. These measures benefit employers but they do nothing for the workers suffering additional years of needless, harmful exposure.

Just the one requirement for a quantitative risk assessment is huge time consuming task. It requires a thorough and detailed review of all animal and human health data to put a number to the actual risk from exposure. It also offers more fodder for opponents to object to. In the case of MC, the quantitative risk assessment is hundreds of pages long and finally ends with, "For an occupational lifetime exposure to 25 ppm MC, OSHA estimates an excess risk of 3.6 MC-induced cancer deaths per 1000 workers."[29] While the finding is useful, is it really necessary to know exactly how many cancer deaths will occur BEFORE protective action is taken? Pretty much, said the United States Supreme Court.

***

The Benzene Decision

In 1976, NIOSH recommended that the benzene PEL be reduced from 10 ppm to 1 ppm to protect the two million exposed workers from benzene-induced leukemia, a cancer of the blood.[30] In 1978, OSHA tried to take NIOSH's advice and was sued by the American Petroleum Institute (producers of benzene) and others, including the AFL-CIO. The case went all the way to the U.S. Supreme Court and the judgment has affected every PEL update attempt since.

During the testimony, OSHA explained its rationale: "There is general agreement that benzene exposure causes leukemia as well as other fatal diseases of the bloodforming organs. In spite of the certainty of this conclusion, there does not exist an adequate scientific basis for establishing the quantitative dose response relationship between exposure to benzene and the induction of leukemia and other blood diseases. The uncertainty in both the actual magnitude of expected deaths and in the theory of extrapolation from existing data to the OSHA exposure levels places the estimation of benefits on 'the frontiers of scientific knowledge.' While the actual estimation of the number of cancers to be prevented is highly uncertain, the evidence indicates that the number may be appreciable."[31]

In other words, the data was strong but incomplete. Meanwhile, OSHA judged a PEL of 1 ppm to be safer than a PEL of 10 ppm. The agency knew that benzene was a carcinogen; industry had not proven what a safe level was; over a million workers were exposed to benzene and they wanted to err on the safe side. OSHA wanted to take the stance that a workplace exposure to known carcinogens should be as low as technologically feasible. It had held hearings on the matter for 17 days and heard from 95 witnesses, including epidemiologists, toxicologists, physicians, political economists, industry representatives, and affected workers.

Three basic opinions were held. Some thought that the proposed PEL of 1 ppm was necessary because benzene exposure would cause material health damage at any level. Others thought 1-ppm was too high and that the evidence showed the PEL should be lower. Some held that the current PEL was adequate and that the benefits were not shown to outweigh the costs.[32] OSHA decided it would go with 1 ppm.

OSHA lost the case. The U.S. Supreme Court decided that the agency needed more evidence to prove significant risk and until they had it, they were required to return to the original 10 ppm PEL.

The aftermath of the benzene decision is that OSHA can only promulgate regulations governing toxic substances when they pose a "significant health risk in the workplace, and that a new, lower standard is therefore reasonably necessary or appropriate to provide safe or healthful employment and places of employment." Industry, on the other hand, does not have to prove significant safety.

"Significant risk" was the death knell for OSHA PELs. Ever since, OSHA has been forced to essentially calculate the exact probability of harm.

Justice Marshall wrote, "Because today's holding has no basis in the Act, and because the Court has no authority to impose

its own regulatory policies on the nation, I dissent."[33] He dis-
agreed with the decision, saying that the Supreme Court had no
right to distort law to conform to their personal views of social
policy.

Justice Marshall felt that the court's interpretation of the
OSHA Act would thwart OSHA's efforts to protect American
workers from cancer and other crippling diseases. He warned
that "existing scientific evidence" might not be enough to meet
the threshold requirement of "significant risk" being imposed by
the Court. His was a call for common sense.

After the defeat, it took OSHA until December of 1987 to
gather the requisite scientific evidence, prove "significant risk
of material impairment," and finally revise the benzene PEL
down to 1 ppm.

How many leukemia's occurred while OSHA spent those 10
additional years gathering boxes of benzene data? How many
lives were lost to the delay? Two professors from Mount Sinai
School of Medicine in New York published a paper on the topic
in *Environmental Health Perspectives*, the respected Journal of the
National Institute of Environmental Health Sciences. Their
results: Out of the 238,000 persons exposed to benzene in seven
industries, between 30 and 490 excess leukemia deaths would
ultimately result from the exposures above 1 ppm occurring
between 1978 and 1987 (death from aplastic anemia and lym-
phoma will make that number higher).[34] In March of 2001, one
of the study's authors—Dr. Philip Landrigan—was a guest pan-
elist on the PBS television special, "Trade Secrets. On the show,
he pin-pointed the excess leukemia death estimate at 492.[35]

The cost of the 1980 Supreme Court's benzene decision goes
far beyond 492 preventable leukemia deaths. The benzene decision set a new criteria for OSHA to meet in order to update
PELs, and the agency has been strangled ever since.

Marching on with its tattered 'to-do-list,' OSHA keeps the
PEL update in its priority plans and sums the drawn-out situa-

tion by saying, "A very large number of workers in a wide variety of occupations and industries are exposed to chemicals at levels known to cause serious health effects; feasible industrial hygiene methods are probably available to reduce these exposures; there is a substantial body of scientific evidence supporting the need for change; and there is considerable support from both business and labor to undertake an effort to address the PELs in a systematic manner."[36] However, OSHA's intentions "to undertake an effort" remain intention, not action.

Justice Marshall was right. The way OSHA is legally bound to update PELs does not work. A decade has passed and OSHA is only in the proposed rule stage for a new PEL process. Benzene, rearing its ugly head yet again, is regulated in 2001 by OSHA at a PEL of 1 ppm while NIOSH recommends 0.1 ppm[37] and ACGIH recommends 0.5 ppm.[38]

Frank Mirer, PhD, CIH of the United Auto Workers described the outrageous PEL situation this way: "PELs fall short because the OSHA standards process is completely derailed. Most of the obstacles are outside the OSHA law, and include: political interference; complex economic analysis required by OMB; threatened and actual appropriations riders; and, the dispirited bureaucracy suffering consequences of years of getting nothing done."[39]

The EPA has identified 2,800 high production chemicals— chemicals produced or imported in quantities exceeding 1 million pounds per year—that lack health data. Only 193 of those 2,800 high production chemicals—less than 7%—have OSHA PELs and most of those are outdated. Hundreds of thousands of chemical exposures occur daily in this country with most of the ill effects wrought by them largely unknown. Not only are the ill effects unknown but the workers suffering them do so unaware of their guinea pig status.

***

Reruns: Perchloroethylene and Hexavalent Chromium

Tragically, history is repeating the senseless MC and benzene stories with new titles like perchloroethylene and hexavalent chromium. Perchloroethylene ('perc' for short) is the most popular dry-cleaning chemical. It causes depression of the central nervous system; damage to the liver and kidneys; confusion; dizziness; headache; drowsiness; and eye, nose, and throat irritation.[40]

One of the chemicals included on the overturned 1988 PEL list, OSHA tried to lower the perc PEL from 100 to 25 ppm. As of 2001, the perc PEL remained at 100 ppm[41] while ACGIH recommends an exposure limit of 25 ppm.

The Halogenated Solvents Industry Alliance (the same that sued to stop the MC PEL revision) represents users and manufacturers of perc. It estimated the U.S. 1998 demand for perc at 344 *million* pounds.[42] The organization argued against the PEL revision in 1988[43] and would likely fight one again.

OSHA estimates that about one million workers are exposed to hexavalent chromium. Used in the production of iron and steel and in electroplating, welding and painting, chromium causes lung cancer, skin ulcers (called chrome holes) and holes in nose cartilage.[44]

The EPA, NIOSH and the International Agency for Research on Cancer have all classified hexavalent chromium as a human carcinogen. In July 1993, the Oil, Chemical, and Atomic Workers International Union and Public Citizen's Health Research Group petitioned OSHA to lower the PEL for hexavalent chromium (CrVI) compounds to 0.5 micrograms per cubic meter of air (ug/m3) from 52 ug/m3. OSHA denied the request.

In April of 1999—six years later—David C. Vladeck, Esq., Director of Public Citizen's Litigation Group (part of the same organization that originally petitioned OSHA in 1993) testified before the Senate Committee on Governmental Affairs on a bill that would add more hoops for OSHA to jump through. In his testimony, Mr. Vladeck described OSHA's ridiculous regulatory process:

> To give you one particularly vivid illustration of the gridlock that now paralyzes our regulatory agencies, let me recount the problems that 200,000 American workers face in having OSHA address the very serious health hazards posed by hexavalent chromium. There is no longer any scientific debate that hexavalent chromium is a potent lung carcinogen. In 1975 and again in 1988, NIOSH urged OSHA to reduce the PEL for hexavalent chromium 100-fold. NIOSH's concern is that the lung cancer risk from hexavalent chromium is intolerably high. OSHA's scientists agree. Their detailed risk assessment shows a range of 88 to 342 excess lung cancer deaths per 1,000 workers exposed to hexavalent chromium levels of half of what is currently permitted over their working lives. This risk is grave by any measure.
>
> What, you ask, has the agency done in the face of a health threat of this magnitude? To date, the answer is nothing. My clients, the Oil, Chemical and Atomic Workers Union and Public Citizen Health Research Group, filed a rulemaking petition with OSHA in 1993 asking the agency to address the health threat posed to workers by hexavalent chromium. Since that time, OSHA has repeatedly acknowledged the gravity of the risk workers are facing, and has pledged to address it swiftly as it can. But the agency, after six years, is still probably at least a year away from publishing a notice of proposed rulemaking. Meanwhile, 200,000 American workers are paying for this regulatory paralysis with their health and well-being.[45]

OSHA's hexavalent chromium PEL still has not changed. Disgusted with the entire process, Drs. Peter Lorie and Sidney

Wolfe from Public Citizen again petitioned Charles Jeffress, the then head of OSHA, to lower the hexavalent chromium PEL. In a July, 11, 2000 letter to Jeffress, they again reviewed the chemical's history and explained how yet another study in the American Journal of Industrial Medicine confirms that hexavalent chromium is a potent lung carcinogen.

Not mincing words, they told Jeffress, "These newly published findings make it clear that your failure to adequately regulate this industrial chemical in a manner consistent with our 1993 petition and 1997 lawsuit to drastically lower workplace exposure levels is in effect a death sentence for thousands of the hundreds of thousands of hexavalent chromium-exposed workers."

The letter concluded, "Five years since the findings of the lung cancer study were first presented, the data are now fully public. The findings are strong, the methods rigorous and the conclusion inescapable: OSHA is guilty of a massive dereliction of duty that has led to the preventable deaths of thousands of workers. Unfortunately, the chromium case is emblematic of the overall pro-industry orientation of OSHA under the Clinton administration. Clinton's OSHA has failed to propose a single new regulation of a hazardous chemical in the seven and a half years it has been in power. (The two regulations it has finalized, methylene chloride and 1,3-butadiene, were first proposed during previous administrations.) If you do not want your administration to go down in history as a massive failure, immediately proposing a rule to regulate chromium is as good a place to start as any."

Still, nothing has been done even though OSHA can establish Emergency Temporary Standards(ETS) when workers are in grave danger and need an ETS to protect them. ETS's are immediately in effect and remain so until superceded by a permanent standard.

In its history, OSHA has passed only nine ETSs. Three were

not challenged and became permanent standards. One was challenged but held up in the court of appeals. Five, however, were stayed or vacated by courts of appeal. According to OSHA, the agency has not issued ETSs in recent years because of the difficulty in meeting the grave danger requirement and proving the need for an immediate, emergency standard.[46] Understandable or not, this ETS acquiescence and the PEL stagnation fails the workforce. For hundreds of thousands of workers, it literally results in death.

OSHA's system of exposure control is not the only area influenced by threat of or actual industry lawsuits. Indeed, it is only one example of OSHA's broken regulatory process.

CHAPTER 6

Olympic Bullying

The Dance of Death: OSHA's Standard Setting Process

While OSHA's mandate is simple, the agency's process of implementing it is not. First, there are multiple sets of OSHA regulations; one for construction; one for general industry; one for maritime and yet another for agriculture. Second, about half the states run their own state OSHA programs so they each have their own set of regulations that are equal to or more stringent than federal OSHA's. Third, government employees are excluded unless states adopt their own laws to protect them. Fourth, the original OSHA Act required word-for-word adoption of existing federal standards and "national consensus standards"—such as those persistent 1968 ANSI exposure limits—as OSHA's first regulations. From the beginning, the agency never had a chance to sit down and properly write its own laws.

After it's requisite 2-year adoption period, OSHA could only pass new regulations through a public participation process, a process where the agency's intentions must be published so interested parties can comment. Interested parties are, for the most part, affected industry groups, unions and professional associations like the ASSE and AIHA. A lawyer explained this stumbling block once by saying, "The agency cannot create, modify or eliminate any standard without going through the lengthy notice-and-comment process. Given its finite resources, OSHA has focused its efforts on adopting new standards instead of revising the standards adopted during its first two years of operation."[1] Many employers, therefore, are still regulated under those cumbersome, initially adopted standards.

An article in the monthly magazine of the AIHA explained OSHA's current regulatory situation this way, "Virtually everyone agrees the existing regulatory standards—standards mandated by a government agency, i.e., OSHA on the federal level—are extremely out-of-date."[2] Hank Lick, the then-president-elect of the AIHA and a business representative to the National Advisory Committee on Occupational Safety and Health said, "There's an anti-regulatory environment in the country today. The pervading atmosphere is that no standard is a good standard." Jim Albers, chair of AIHA's Social Concerns Committee, explained, "Since OSHA's inception and in response to business opposition, all three branches of government have acted to reduce OSHA's standard-setting authority."[3]

The existing process that federal OSHA must go through to pass regulations, the agency's lack of resources, and the lack of public and Congressional support have left the agency's rulebook with too many problems to count.

When OSHA tries to update an individual PEL, for example, affected industries and industry associations work hard to delay it. Usually, those industries are well financed and politically influential. For instance, the Halogenated Solvents Industry Association (HSIA) filed suit against OSHA to halt the revision of the MC standard. The HSIA represents companies that manufacture and use MC, big companies like The Dow Chemical Company and Vulcan Materials Company— and it doesn't have to fight OSHA on all its PELs, just the halogenated solvents like MC and perc. So they focus their plentiful lawyers, funds, research, and experts on OSHA and its attempt to update one or two PEL.

This scenario plays out well beyond the PEL issue. When OSHA proposes new standards or tries to revise an existing one, affected industries sue the agency. In some cases, like the 1989 PEL update, the unions also sue OSHA for not being protective enough. The result is inadequate protection and an OSHA drained of its limited, taxpayer funded resources. The agency can't afford to respond in kind for every PEL attempt and every new regulation.

Congress itself puts major stumbling blocks in front of OSHA progress. According to Charles Lewis, who wrote about the matter is his 1998 book *The Buying of the Congress*, "OSHA has always been hampered when it comes to developing, passing, and enforcing regulations and safety standards to protect American workers. And the entity that has constricted it has been Congress. Treating it as the federal government's favorite whipping boy, Congress and big business have spent twenty-eight years emasculating the agency rather than helping it create a better working environment for all. Together they have shaped the agency's image from one of protector of American working men and women to one of meddler in company business."[4]

For several years, for instance, Congress refused to allow OSHA to issue an ergonomics standard by literally banning it as a stipulation (called a rider) in their annual budget. Ergonomics may not seem as important as electrocution hazards or heavy equipment safety but, according to most estimates, it is the biggest occupational injury and illness problem in the United States today. Every year, one-third of all occupational injuries and illnesses reported to the Bureau of Labor Statistics (BLS) are work-related musculoskeletal disorders, the kind an ergonomic standard would address.

When OSHA persisted and finally proposed an ergonomic standard, the serious army of industry groups fighting it did not hesitate to show their teeth. Occupational Hazards magazine forewarned of the looming battle saying "Attorneys representing the U.S. Chamber of Commerce, the National Coalition on Ergonomics, the National Association of Manufacturers and other business groups blasted away at the scientific foundations of the standard, its provisions and the process OSHA is following to promulgate it. The Chamber has threatened to take OSHA to court if the agency proceeds with the rule, and procedural complaints could be useful in a future legal challenge."[5]

Industry threats to sue OSHA are more than threats. They are guarantees. Within the immediate days and weeks that followed OSHA's final ergonomic standard, lawsuits against OSHA piled up. Four major unions sued to try to strengthen certain parts of it but they were overwhelmingly outnumbered, as was OSHA. The National Coalition on Ergonomics, a huge group of industries banding together to oppose the standard, documented the legal filings on it's website—the logjam that formed within only two months illustrates what OSHA is up against, and who.

PETITIONS FOR REVIEW FILED OR ANTICIPATED (as of 1/4/01)

National Association of Manufacturers v. Occupational Safety & Health Administration and Secretary of Labor (No. 00-1473, D.C. Cir.) (filed 11/8/00)

Chamber of Commerce of the United States of America, LPA, Inc., National Beer Wholesalers Association, and Society for Human Resource Management v. Occupational Safety & Health Administration and Secretary of Labor (No. 00-1477, D.C. Cir.) (filed 11/13/00) (consolidated with *NAM v. OSHA* on 11/14/00).

Atlantic Indemnity Co. et al. v. Herman (No. 00-2461, 4th Cir., filed 11/14) (167 companies listed as petitioners, under the auspices of the American Insurance Association).

National Coalition on Ergonomics, Air Conditioning Contractors of America, Alliance of American Insurers, American Association for Homecare, Inc., American Bakers Association, American Coke and Coal Chemicals Institute, American Flange and Manufacturing Co., Inc., American Hardware Manufacturers Association, American Hotel and Motel Association, American

Meat Institute, American Moving and Storage Association, American Road & Transportation Builders Association, American Supply Association, Anheuser-Busch Companies, Inc., Automotive Oil Change Association, Copper and Brass Fabricators Council, Corn Refiners Association, Dayton Area Chamber of Commerce, Federal Express Corporation, FedEx Ground Package System, Inc., The Ferroalloys Association, Fitzpatrick & Weller, Inc., Florida Beer Wholesalers Association, Food Distributors International, Food Marketing Institute, Grocery Manufacturers of America, Inc., Harris Corporation, IPC International, Inc., Independent Bakers Association, International Bottled Water Association, International Fabricare Institute, International Mass Retail Association, International Sanitary Supply Association, International Warehouse Logistics Association, Kitchen Cabinet Manufacturers Association, Manufactured Housing Institute, Manufacturing Jewelers and Suppliers of America, National Association of Chain Drug Stores, National Association of Wholesalers-Distributors, National Club Association, National Grocers Association, National Home Furnishings Association, National Oilseed Processors Association, National Roofing Contractors Association, National Soft Drink Association, National Turkey Federation, National Utility Contractors Association, Non-Ferrous Founders' Society, North Coast Container Corp., Precision Metal Forming Association, Promotional Products Association International, Rubber Manufacturers Association, Small Business Legislative Council, Snack Food Association, South Carolina Chamber of Commerce, Steel Shipping Container Institute, Textile Rental Services Association, Tire Association of North America, Uniform and Textile Services Association, United Parcel Service, Inc., Viking Freight, Inc., Wine and Spirits Wholesalers of America, and Wood Machinery Manufacturers of America v. OSHA (No. 00-1490, D.C. Cir., filed 11/20, consolidated with NAM v. OSHA on 11/22/00)

United Steelworkers of America v. OSHA (No. 00-3849, 3d

Cir., filed 11/17/00)

UNITE (Union of Needletrades, Industrial & Textile Employees) v. OSHA (No. 00-4237, 2d Cir., filed 11/17/00)

AFL-CIO (No. 00-2434, 1st Cir., filed 11/17/00)

International Brotherhood of Teamsters (No. 00-71519, 9th Cir., filed 11/20/00)

Oregon AFL-CIO v. OSHA (No. 00-71529, 9th Cir., filed 11/14/00)

United Food and Commercial Workers International Union v. OSHA (No. 00-2448, 1st Cir., filed 11/22/00)

American Iron and Steel Institute (No. 00-60823, 5th Cir., filed 11/22/00)

The Newspaper Association of America (filed its petition for review 12/13/00)

Motor & Equipment Manufacturers Association and *Original Equipment Suppliers Association v. OSHA* (filed its petition for review 12/19/00)

American Moving & Storage Association, Inc. v. OSHA (No. 00-1493, D.C. Cir., consolidated with *NAM v. OSHA* on 11/22/00.

Computing Technology Industry Association v. OSHA (No. 00-1519, D.C. Cir., consolidated with *NAM v. OSHA* on 12/8/00)

Distribution & LTL Carriers Assn., Inc. v. OSHA. (No. 00-1504, D.C. Cir., consolidated with *NAM v. OSHA* on 11/30/00)

Washington Legal Foundation (No. 00-1520, D.C. Cir., consolidated with *NAM v. OSHA* on 12/8/00).

Edison Electric Institute and National Rural Electric Cooperative Association v. OSHA (filed 12/28/00, D.C. Cir.).

American Trucking Associations v. OSHA (filed 12/29/00, D.C. Cir.).

Additional petitioners to be consolidated with NAM/NCE suit (planning to file in D.C. Cir.)[6]

(More on ergonomics in chapter 7)

The real casualties of these expensive, drawn out political battles are the workers. In OSHA's estimation, the 1989 PEL update alone would have provided additional health protection for over 21 million employees; eliminated 55,000 occupational illnesses and 683 deaths each year.[7] Taxpaying workers pay with their health, and they financially support the court system, OSHA agency and Congress so tied up and gagged by special interest groups.

The process has degraded into a contest of who can afford the most lawyers and which battles to invest in—a predictable dance of legal maneuverings. OSHA can't afford to fight for each and every standard; the agency is a perennial underdog, lacking in funds, stature and support. The result: OSHA regulations—and therefore workplace safety and health conditions—are based on politics instead of science, health and desirable social policy.

***

Beryllium

Beryllium is a metal used for nuclear weapons, atomic energy, and in metal alloys for dental appliances, golf clubs, nonsparking tools, and wheel chairs. It's a useful metal because it weighs little but is stronger than steel. It also happens to cause cancer and chronic beryllium disease (CBD) — a fatal, suffocating disease where the lungs scar so badly they can't dissolve oxygen into the blood. There is no cure.

Workers at Brush Wellman in Tucson, Arizona make electronic parts. At the Tuscon plant, 25 workers have the disease. Company-wide, the number stricken climbs to 141.[8] The tragedy of Brush Wellman is that it could have been prevented.

According to an investigative report published in the Arizona Daily Star, "...the Ohio-based company moved the most dangerous part of its beryllium business to Tucson just as it helped kill a federal safety plan that could have reduced the hazard." The report explains that when OSHA tried to lower the beryllium PEL in the mid-1970's, "The company called in its heavyweight customers—the Departments of Defense and Energy. Together, they defeated the tougher standard."[9]

The report explains Brush's 1970's tactics; they mirror those used today. Brush attacked the science supporting the reduction, arguing that workers were already adequately protected, and they called on powerful allies in government, specifically the U. S. Department of Energy and the Department of Defense.[10]

Today, despite 141 seriously ill workers, Brush still steadfastly asserts that there is no conclusive evidence to show the standard isn't working.[11] The newspaper reported, "Brush officials see no contradiction in saying the federal standard is safe even while workers get sick. Their explanation, "Workers might have been exposed to levels higher than the safety limit during accidents."[12]

Several years earlier, Dr. Sandra Steingraber quoted a long-time employee in OSHA's health standards department, Dr. Peter Infante, in Living Downstream—her book on cancer and the environment. In a discussion on the struggles of regulating workplace carcinogens, she quoted the frustrated advocate of workplace health as saying, "'We need more study' is the grandfather of all arguments for taking no action."[13]

In 1977, Dr. Infante sat in a public hearing and personally heard his then-boss Edward Baier from NIOSH testify to OSHA, "Probably no compounds known to man give so consistent a carcinogenic response in so many animal species as do the compounds of beryllium....Some beryllium compounds have been shown to cause lung cancer at doses lower than that for any other pulmonary carcinogen."[14] Dr. Infante had even co-authored a report on beryllium death patterns, which supported his boss's testimony.

More than twenty years later, OSHA's Dr. Infante was quoted in the Arizona Daily Star saying, "Apparently there was this concerted effort by Brush to stop the standard and they were successful. And now, as a society, we're paying the price for that. Can you imagine how I feel as an employee of a regulatory agency every time I see one of these workers with chronic beryllium disease who are going to suffocate to death from this disease?"

In the United States, there are about 30,000 workers in 8,000 plants who may be potentially exposed to beryllium.[15] The OSHA beryllium standard is the same today as it was thirty years ago. Recently, the Paper, Allied-Industrial, Chemical and Energy Workers Union(PACE) petitioned OSHA to issue an emergency temporary standard to protect workers from CBD and lung cancer from beryllium. OSHA denied it. The issue is now parked as a line item on the OSHA priority list. It's been there five years already.

Meanwhile, beryllium-sensitized workers convert to CBD at an estimated rate of 10 percent per year. Recent study results indicate that between 5 percent and 15 percent of beryllium-exposed workers are sensitized and will eventually develop CBD.[16]

***

The Dance Steps: OSHA Initiatives and Industry Attacks

OSHA's Cooperative Compliance Program

In 1997, OSHA wrote a directive outlining a new approach to best use its resources. Called the Cooperative Compliance Program (CCP), the program would have allowed OSHA to avoid inspecting safe business while targeting employers with injury and illness rates double or higher than the national rate. Employers with high injury and illness rates could voluntarily comply with OSHA and implement comprehensive safety and health programs or else face the threat of an OSHA inspection—something they are already subject to.

A group of industry associations, including heavy hitters like the U.S. Chamber of Commerce, the National Association of Manufacturers, the American Trucking Association, and the Food Marketing Institute, sued OSHA. Industry claimed the CCP was a rule and that OSHA was required to use notice-and-comment rulemaking pursuant to the Administrative Procedure Act. Industry won and forced the agency to stop the CCP.

The U.S Court of Appeals for the District of Columbia found that OSHA should have issued the CCP as a rule. In order to do that, OSHA would have to go through its lengthy notice and comment period and prove "significant risk" (not likely over an inspection procedure), only to be sued again over the final product. Instead, OSHA reverted back to its traditional inspection procedures for workplaces with high injury and illness rates.

OSHA's Safety and Health Program Standard

If OSHA wrote rules regulating every hazard in all types of industries for all kinds of chemicals and procedures, there would be no book large enough to hold all the pages. So, the agency tried to promulgate a general safety and health program standard that was simple and results oriented. OSHA described what employers should have and employers could decide how to get there. Voluntary guidelines were issued in 1989, and after years of stakeholder meetings, OSHA finally proposed a draft of its health and safety program standard in 1998. It required regulated employers to develop an overall safety and health program to address five things: management leadership and employee participation; hazard identification and assessment; hazard prevention and control; information and training; and evaluation of program effectiveness.

At the time, OSHA's acting deputy director of policy, and director of the Office of Regulatory Analysis, Marthe Kent, said," If OSHA had it to do over again, this would probably be the first standard we would promulgate, because it truly provides employers and employees with the foundation for workplace safety and health. OSHA also believes that this standard has the potential to reach those workplaces (especially small workplaces) that we have traditionally had difficulty reaching. That's why we're planning a massive outreach effort to support this standard, including checklists, an expert system, model programs, training materials and small entity compliance guides. In terms of the standard's potential impact, our evidence suggests that companies that implement effective safety and health programs can expect reductions of 20% or greater in their injury and illness rates and a return of $4 to $6 for every $1 invested in the program."[17]

The response from the U.S. Chamber of Commerce was proudly announced in their March 23, 1999 press release titled, "U.S. Chamber Blasts Safety and Health Proposal: Vague New Policy Would Expose Business to Major Workplace Liability." The U.S. Chamber organized testimony before the U.S. House Subcommittee on Workforce Protections as part of an industry group calling themselves the Alliance for Workplace Safety. Safety, however, was nowhere to be found in the comment made by the U.S. Chamber's vice president of labor policy who predictably claimed that small businesses will be "particularly hurt" and said of the rule, "It requires employers to identify and address workplace hazards on a continuous basis, while not providing any benchmark standards of compliance."

Explaining their opinion to Congress, the U.S. Chamber said the proposed Safety and Health Program Rule "would open companies everywhere to unlimited workplace liability and allow OSHA to circumvent its own rulemaking requirements."[18] Although the Chamber's press release pushed the fear-invoking liability and cost buttons, it failed to note that the safety and health program rule could improve workplace conditions and reduce injuries and illnesses.

The testimony of Mr. Lawrence P. Halprin, Partner at Keller & Heckman, LLP to the United States House of Representatives Committee on Small Business illustrates the legal microscope held by OSHA's opposition. While industry lawyers usually bemoan OSHA's "One size fits all" approach, here, Mr. Halprin complained that OSHA did not specify requirements in sufficient detail, leaving too much discretion to compliance officers. OSHA was trying to leave discretion to the employers. In part, Mr. Halprin said:

"There are three fundamental principles which must constantly be kept in mind when evaluating this OSHA initiative:

First, the generally held view that an effective safety and health program can be expected to significantly improve workplace safety does not mean that an OSHA mandated program will have that effect.

Second, regardless of the benefits which may be derived from a government mandate, that mandate is impermissible if it entrusts Constitutional Due Process to the whims of a compliance officer or otherwise exceeds the scope of the agency's delegated authority.

Third, direct government regulation should be minimized or avoided when there are alternative mechanisms for achieving the same objective. Applying those principles, we have at least four fundamental objections to OSHA's draft SHPR:

1) First, while we do not believe the rule would significantly improve workplace safety and health in the United States, it would cost employers billions of dollars each year;

2) Second, as presently drafted and in the absence of a fundamental paring back of its scope and requirements, we believe the SHPR violates the fundamental Constitutional principles of Due Process because it fails to provide employers with adequate notice as to what is required or to place any meaningful limits on the discretion of compliance personnel;

3) Third, we believe OSHA lacks the legal authority under the OSH Act to issue the SHPR as a final rule— whether as a standard or as a regulation— because:

a) we believe the recent D.C. Circuit decision in the CCP case makes it clear that, if OSHA has the legal authority to adopt the SHPR, it can do so only through the process for adopting standards and not regulations;

b) we believe the application of a SHP standard to the hazards covered by the General Duty Clause constitutes an invalid attempt to amend the General Duty Clause outside the legislative process; and

c) we believe the application of a SHP standard to all of the hazards covered by existing OSHA standards constitutes an unauthorized effort to amend those standards or otherwise regulate the covered hazards through a generic rulemaking contrary to the requirements of the OSH Act and the 11th Circuit decision in the 1989 PELs case which vacated OSHA's attempt to establish or amend approximately 400 permissible exposure limits through a generic rulemaking.

4) Fourth, the SHPR would inject a meddling government bureaucracy into the financial and labor-management decision-making process of every employer in the United States—a role for which it is particularly ill-suited.

For these reasons, which are more fully developed and explained in my written statement, we believe adoption of a rule substantially along the lines of the draft SHPR would be both illegal and clearly contrary to public policy."[19]

Industry's exhaustive legal and political wrangling won again. To date, OSHA has not passed a safety and health program standard. It is not because the benefits from a comprehensive health and safety program are unknown; companies have voluntarily implemented them for years as part of OSHA's Voluntary Protection Program with proven success in accident prevention. Rather, the safety and health program rule won't become a requirement because OSHA and improved worker welfare are simply no match for the opposition.

The Savagery of Attack—
OSHA's Home Inspection Nightmare

Industry and political opponents of OSHA like to portray OSHA as a bunch of bureaucratic extremists. During the blood-borne pathogens debate, for example, an inflammatory and misleading interpretation spread by opponents and picked up by the press was how OSHA would make the tooth fairy illegal by regulating children's teeth as hazardous.[20] During the ergonomics debate, comments were made about how OSHA would require employers to pay for golfing injuries.

On November 15, 1999, OSHA issued a letter explaining its management practice for home work environments. The interpretive letter was requested by an employer with sales executives in home offices instead of commercial office buildings. OSHA took two years to carefully write the six-page letter to address all home work scenarios, not just home office environments. Among other things, the letter said:

"OSHA's health and safety inspection program is directed primarily toward industrial and commercial establishments and construction sites. We do not ordinarily conduct inspections of home-based workplaces, although from time to time we have visited private homes or apartments to investigate reports of sweatshop-type working conditions in the garment industry and other businesses. We would also investigate work-related fatalities occurring in home-based workplaces. Any OSHA enforcement visit must, of course, be conducted in compliance with the Fourth Amendment which would require that OSHA obtain either consent to inspect or a judicially-issued warrant."[21] Clearly, OSHA was not planning to barge into home offices. On a practical level, neither federal or state OSHA's have the budgets to expand their inspection scope into people's homes.

Regarding whether OSHA expected employers to inspect home office environments, the letter explained,

> "There is no general requirement in OSHA's standards or regulations that employers routinely conduct safety inspections of all work locations. However, certain specific standards require periodic inspection of specific kinds of equipment and work operations, such as: ladders....compressed gas cylinders....electrical protective equipment....mechanical power-transmission equipment....resistance welding....portable electric equipment..."[22]

This is not the same as saying home offices should be inspected.

OSHA further explained, "The OSHA Act applies to work performed by an employee in any workplace within the United States, including a workplace located in the employee's home," and immediately clarified, in the next paragraph, what that meant in the practical sense. "Even when the workplace is in a designated area in an employee's home, the employer retains some degree of control over the conditions of the "work at home" agreement. An important factor in the development of these arrangements is to ensure that employees are not exposed to *reasonably foreseeable hazards* (italics added) created by their at-home employment...." This makes sense. If an employer sends an employee home with a computer, it is logical to instruct them on how to ergonomically position their home work station. Employers already do this in commercial workspaces. Likewise, if employees are sent home with raw materials like adhesives or paints, providing gloves and chemical information is appropriate.

OSHA's phrase "reasonably foreseeable hazards" excludes threats from children's toys left on the stairs and grumpy dogs. Still, Pat Cleary, vice president of human resources at the National Association of Manufacturers, said, "This is nuts.

They're trying to match a 30-year-old law with a year 2000 work force. The law doesn't contemplate everyone painting their banisters yellow."[23]

The same OSHA letter went on, "Ensuring safe and healthful working conditions for the employee should be a precondition for any home-based work assignments. Employers should exercise reasonable diligence to identify in advance the possible hazards..."

Despite use of words like "reasonable diligence" and "reasonably foreseeable hazards", the result was a feeding frenzy with OSHA portrayed as the ruin of telecommuting, the harbinger of auto pollution, and the catalyst for less family time and home business bankruptcy. OSHA opponents ran with stories of how OSHA would knock on front doors and require things like exit signs and nailing down throw rugs. The American Industrial Hygiene Association (AIHA) monthly magazine, The Synergist, described the unexpected OSHA attack as "a political windfall for those seeking re-election—an issue that constituents understand and will make great "talk" on the campaign trail."[24] At least four bills were introduced into Congress to prevent OSHA from inspecting home work environments. Three weeks later, the House subcommittee on investigations and oversight held a hearing to look into the policy. Republican Representative Bob Schaffer of Colorado said Charles Jeffress, the head of OSHA at the time, should resign if he did not determine who was responsible.[25] Another Republican Representative, David McIntosh of Indiana, scheduled a hearing called, "Is the Department of Labor Regulating the Public Through the Back Door?" The ABC News show 20/20 ran a segment on the issue, unabashedly giving it the biased title of "Give me a Break" which invoked comment from the AIHA.[26]

There are serious health and safety risks for thousands of low, paid-by-the-piece workers given chemicals and machinery and told to return with finished products. Unheard above the political clamor were worker voices, like those of piece-workers in California's silicon valley making circuits with lead, acids and fluxes at their kitchen tables and in their bathrooms.[27] Not only were the real safety and health issues of home-based work ignored, they were publicly beaten into a non-issue.

A May, 1997 special supplement to the BLS's Current Population Survey estimated that more than 21 million persons did some part of their primary job at home. While 9 out of 10 home workers were deemed "white-collar," about 1.6 million service workers and more than half a million manufacturing workers were paid for work from home. According to the BLS, "All of the major industry groups except mining had significant numbers of workers doing paid work at home."[28] With current economic trends, these numbers can only be expected to grow.

In its initial home inspection letter, OSHA had laid out reasonable expectations and guidance to meet the already established mandate in the OSHA Act "to assure so far as possible safe and healthful working conditions."[29] OSHA was not adding a new burden onto employers but advising them on how to best meet their existing obligations with the changing workplace. This never made the press.

The political onslaught was too great and on January 5, 2000, OSHA publicly retracted its interpretive letter. Six-weeks later, OSHA quietly published a guideline for its compliance officers on home-based worksites. In it, the badly beaten agency first mumbled the mantra whipped into it about supporting "family-friendly, flexible and fair work arrangements" which most OSHA personnel probably believed in the first place. The policy section, the end result of the political home inspection firestorm, contains the real wreckage. It says:

"OSHA will not conduct inspections of employees' home offices (defined as writing, computer work and such). OSHA will not hold employers liable for employees' home offices, and does not expect employers to inspect the home offices of their employees.

If OSHA receives a complaint about a home office, the complainant will be advised of OSHA's policy. If an employee specifically requests, OSHA may let the employer know of the complaint but will not follow up."[30]

Employees sitting in a commercial office building are now more protected than those doing the same jobs while sitting in their homes. With the threat of OSHA inspection gone and no ergonomics regulation to follow, employers can save the costs of ergonomic chairs, keyboards, phone headsets, and surveys by moving employees into their homes. In fact, there is now financial incentive to move workers from carpal-tunnel riddled workplaces into their homes.

To make matters worse, if an employee complains, OSHA cannot act. The policy section states that OSHA will inspect other home-based worksites, such as manufacturing, only "when OSHA receives a complaint or referral that indicates that a violation of a safety or health standard exists that threatens physical harm, or that an imminent danger exists, including reports of a work-related fatality." In other words, OSHA will look away from home-based worksites unless they are somehow shown that a serious or life-threatening hazard exists there.

Buried in the policy section of OSHA Instruction CPL 2-0.125 is true distortion of the OSHA Act. But no outcry arose. No Congressional hearings were demanded to determine, "Is the Department of Labor Regulating the Public Through the Back Door?" No "Give Me A Break" shows aired. Apparently, back door regulating is acceptable when the pendulum of responsibility swings away from the employer.

Fighting Voluntary Guidelines

Explaining to AIHA members why the organization was becoming more involved in voluntary standards, such as those established by the non-profit American National Standards Institute (ANSI), AIHA president-elect Henry Lick said, "The groups that oppose OSHA standards are raising the same issues with ANSI standards." The article quoting Lick went further to explain why members should expect resistance to their efforts: "Those organizations fear OSHA will default to a general-duty clause and invoke an ANSI standard, so they expend time and money to keep ANSI standards from passing as well. But the voluntary process is still a significant improvement over the stalled regulatory process."[31]

The general-duty clause is a section of the original OSHA act, commonly referred to as the (5)(a)(1) clause due to its location in the Act. It was intended to grant OSHA the ability to regulate hazards that were not specifically regulated under a standard or regulation, like those "reasonably foreseeable hazards" referred to in the home inspection letter. The (5)(a)(1) clause does not give OSHA free reign, however, because (5)(a)(1) citations are only issued where there is a serious and recognized hazard which can be feasibly abated.[32] This has been the law since OSHA's inception.

An employer could be cited under the general-duty clause, for example, if they over-expose an employee to a chemical not regulated by OSHA but one which the employer has toxicity information on. The employer must know of the hazard and the hazard must be serious for OSHA to cite the general-duty clause.

So, industry is afraid of voluntary guidelines because it views them as supporting documentation for general-duty citations and as the next step to a regulation. How fearful is industry of voluntary guidelines? In his best-selling nonfiction book on the fast food restaurant industry, Fast Food Nation, Eric Schlosser described OSHA's efforts to address the growing threat of workplace violence.

> OSHA attempted in the mid-1990's to issue guidelines for preventing violence at restaurants and stores that do business at night. OSHA was

prompted, among other things, by the fact that homicide had become the leading cause of workplace fatalities among women. The proposed guidelines were entirely voluntary and seemed innocuous. OSHA recommended, for example, that late-night retailers improve visibility within their stores and make sure their parking lots were well lit. The National Restaurant Association (NRA), along with other industry groups, responded by enlisting more than one hundred congressmen to oppose any OSHA guidelines on retail violence. An investigation by the Los Angeles Times found that many of these congressmen had recently accepted donations from the NRA and the National Association of Convenience Stores.[33]

Did OSHA go nuts writing violations after issuing voluntary guidelines on workplace violence? No. Federal OSHA has no regulations governing workplace violence, and the agency has not issued any general duty clause citations for workplace violence since March, 1995. In fact, only ten employers were ever cited for workplace violence and all the citations occurred prior to the issuance of the voluntary compliance guidelines.[34]

No government agency, including OSHA, has the money and expertise to write laws to cover each and every possible scenario that may arise. Thankfully, there are qualified organizations offering voluntary guidelines and recommendations. Called consensus standards, these voluntary guidelines are coming under increasing attack by industry.

The international, nonprofit National Fire Protection Association (NFPA) began in 1896 to reduce the worldwide burden of fire and other hazards. Today, the organization has a membership of 69,000 with more than 6,000 voluntary representatives serving on 250 technical committees.[35] The NFPA's

Life Safety Code for example, gives specific and detailed infor-mation that OSHA cannot possibly replicate. One nugget from this book for conscientious health care facilities is: "The mini-mum clear width for doors in the means of egress from hospitals, nursing homes, limited care facilities and psychiatric hospital sleeping rooms, and diagnostic and treatment areas such as X-ray, surgery, or physical therapy shall be at least 32 inches (81 cm) wide."[36]

For more than 80 years, ANSI has served as administrator and coordinator of private industry's voluntary standardization system, consensus standards. ANSI itself does not develop stan-dards; rather, its job is to ensure that the 175 ANSI-accredited organizations, such as the NFPA, follow the ANSI guiding prin-ciples of consensus, due process and openness in developing standards in their areas of expertise. In 1999, the total number of approved American National Standards reached 14,650.[37] Two worked on by the AIHA include Ventilation and Operation of Open-Surface Tanks and Fundamentals Governing the Design and Operation of Local Exhaust Systems.[38]

Consensus standards are a valuable and necessary tool for our country to remain competitive and technologically advanced. We face the risk, however, of losing control of our basic rights by turning over authorship of our nation's laws to parties with private interests. Compound the steep, national trend towards consensus standards with OSHA's beleaguered rulemaking process and the nation could lose what's left of the integrity of OSHA protections.

So far, industry completely outweighs OSHA in representa-tion on consensus setting committees. OSHA has only 50 staffers participating as members on consensus standards com-mittees.[39]

Because of the government's intentional, increased reliance on consensus standards, industry has a vested interest in controlling those standards. The reason industry scrutinizes consensus standards can be found in an October 20, 1993 memo from the federal Office of Management and Budget (OMB).[40] This memo serves as the policy for the government's use of consensus standards and requires all federal agencies to use voluntary consensus standards in lieu of government-unique standards except where inconsistent with law or otherwise impractical. OMB means business; if an agency does not want to adopt a voluntary consensus standard, they must submit a report explaining why to both the OMB and the National Institute of Standards and Technology (NIST).

The OMB requires the use of consensus standards because they:

- Eliminate the cost to the Government of developing its own standards and decrease the cost of goods procured and the burden of complying with agency regulation.

- Provide incentives and opportunities to establish standards that serve national needs.

- Encourage long-term growth for U.S. enterprises and promote efficiency and economic competition through harmonization of standards

- Further the policy of reliance upon the private sector to supply Government needs for goods and services. [41]

The problem is that industry has become so giddy with power that they are now reaching forcefully to control all aspects of the occupational health and safety scene, including voluntary standards. In 2000, the legal bullying reached a new depth as ACGIH was sued for the first time in its 62-year history.

In a move shocking to even the most seasoned skeptics, ACGIH was sued by the Refractory Ceramic Fibers (RCF) Coalition, Thermal Ceramics, Inc., Unifrax Corporation, and the Vesuvius U.S.A. Corporation. These plaintiffs alleged that

ACGIH is a standard-setting organization, and that the ACGIH exposure limit for RCF is unreasonable and unjustified. They argued that their own Recommended Exposure Guideline is adequate. The suit also argued that there is a conflict of interest due to the involvement in the ACGIH process of federal employees and employees of labor unions. The plaintiffs wanted the court to stop ACGIH from studying RCF and from publishing its recommended exposure limit. Shamelessly, they even sought substantial monetary damages.

Not surprisingly, the RCFC recommended exposure limit is higher than that recommended by ACGIH. In fact, it is two and a half times higher.[42] OSHA, on the other hand, has no exposure limit for RCF. Approximately 800 workers manufacture RCFs and about 31,500 more install and handle products containing RCFs.[43] In its 2001 listing of exposure limits, ACGIH cites cancer and lung fibrosis as the basis of their exposure limit.[44]

The ACGIH has always printed in the inside cover of its exposure booklet a policy statement warning users that the exposure limits are "*not* fine lines between safety and dangerous concentrations and *should not* be used by anyone untrained in the discipline of industrial hygiene."[45] This was not enough for the RCFC plaintiffs who agreed to dismiss the ACGIH/RCFC lawsuit based on ACGIH publishing a press release further clarifying its exposure limit. Driving legal inroads into the ACGIH process, the embattled organization "clarified," its formerly clear policy statement with the following mumbo-jumbo: "No TLV, including the TLV for refractory ceramic fibers, represents a judgment that other exposure guidelines, which may be based on other parameters, are appropriate or inappropriate....ACGIH recognizes that other not-for-profit organizations, industry, and individual companies also develop and recommend workplace health and safety guidelines. Examples of such guidelines are those of the American

Industrial Hygiene Association, the National Fire Protection Association, RCFC, and many individual companies such as Dow, Dupont, Merck, and ExxonMobil. ACGIH encourages and commends any such guidelines that are based on credible health science, undertaken with a process that includes rigorous, independent wide-spread peer review and that help to protect workers from hazardous exposures. The guidelines developed by others, such as those noted above, are sometimes more restrictive that the TLVs and sometimes less restrictive...."

This loud shot across the bow concluded with ACGIH publicly stating, "RCFC has advised ACGIH that it has developed additional data regarding RCF, and will be submitting that data for review by ACGIH. ACGIH has agreed to review this data."[46] What exactly does this mean? ACGIH already considers all applicable data when recommending exposure limits, and RCFC-supported science can hardly be considered unbiased. Will the volunteer committee at ACGIH feel pressure to weigh this data more heavily than it would have before the expensive, legal bullying? What is the future cost of the precedent set by ACGIH's "clarification" of the TLVs? Murky is the slow, creeping damage produced by the pressure of industry lawsuits unchecked by the public and Congress.

During the same month ACGIH was hit with the RCFC lawsuit (December, 2000), another industry group sued the agency. This time, the plaintiffs were: Anchor Glass Container Corp; FMC Corporation; The General Chemical Group, Inc.; OCI Chemical Corporation; Solvay Minerals; and the Wyoming Mining Association. These producers and users of Sodium sesquicarbonate (nicknamed trona) sought to prohibit ACGIH from publishing a trona exposure limit. The suit went so far as to try to stop the ACGIH from even holding meetings to discuss trona, arguing that ACGIH is a quasi-governmental, standard-setting organization. The Department of Labor (OSHA), and the Department of Health and Human Services

(NIOSH) were also sued because of their alleged reliance upon, and use of TLVs, and because employees of OSHA, MSHA, and NIOSH are members of ACGIH.[47] The suit alleged that publication of the ACGIH trona exposure limit would mislead employees and consumers about safe levels of trona exposure, and that the plaintiffs would be irreparably damaged. They too sought monetary damages from the non-profit ACGIH.

According to the Wyoming Mining Association's website, "Wyoming's Trona industry produced over 17.2 million tons, employing 2,882 mine and processing plant workers in 1998. All Wyoming trona is mined underground. The trona is mined, then processed into soda ash or bicarbonate of soda. Wyoming has the world's largest deposit of trona, and supplies about 90% of the nation's soda ash."[48]

The ACGIH intended to recommend a trona exposure limit of 0.5 milligrams of respirable trona dust per cubic meter of air based on irritation and lung function effects.[49] Ironically, one of the plaintiffs (Solvay Minerals, Inc.) own Material Safety Data Sheet (MSDS) for trona listed inhalation, skin contact and ingestion as hazardous routes of exposure and warned that trona is an alkaline product that will irritate digestive mucous membranes, eyes and healthy skin. Specifically, it listed the following effects of exposure:

Inhalation (dust): May be irritating to the nose, throat, and respiratory tract. Repeated exposure may cause nosebleeds.

Eyes: May cause irritation, severe watering and redness.

Skin: May cause skin irritation, seen as redness and swelling. In the presence of moisture or sweat, irritation may become more severe leading to rash.

Ingestion: May cause gastrointestinal irritation including nausea, vomiting, abdominal cramps, and diarrhea. May cause irritation of the mouth and throat.[50]

Revising its MSDS just seven months before the lawsuit, Solvay Minerals voluntarily listed the ACGIH's exposure limits on its own MSDS for customers everywhere to use. Why? Because seven months earlier, the ACGIH did not have a specific exposure limit for trona so the general dust limit of 10 milligrams per cubic meter was applicable. That was apparently acceptable. After the ACGIH noted its intent to publish a trona-specific limit of 0.5 milligrams per cubic meter, the plaintiffs—including Solvay Minerals—accused ACGIH of being an unacceptable quasi-governmental, standard-setting organization.

OSHA has no specific exposure limit for trona so it falls under the general nuisance dust limit of 15 milligrams per cubic meter. In other words, OSHA regulates trona in a mine the same as dirt on a construction site. If voluntary organizations like ACGIH are stopped from publishing recommended exposure limits, workers would basically be left with only OSHA's inadequate exposure limits or those set by manufacturers.

The trona lawsuit was settled out of court with the ACGIH removing its intended new limit for trona. ACGIH also agreed to wait for a study from the same organizations that produce trona and sued the agency. But perhaps the worst evidence of the bruising bullying can be found in the legalistic language the ACGIH released in its public statement after the settlement:

> ACGIH agrees that while there is evidence of irritation caused by exposure to any dust at some threshold level, there is no evidence at this time of health effects, other than a potential transient irritant effect, from exposure to trona. ACGIH further agrees that the publication of its TLV for

trona on the Notice of Intended Change list was preliminary and was never meant to communicate that there was a scientific basis at this time that exposure to trona causes health effects, other than a potential transient irritant effect.[51]

ACGIH is not a concensus building organization but a technical one. While it is not perfect, its goal has been to publish what it believes to be scientifically valid and responsible. After these two lawsuits, ACGIH is now issuing public statements based on language approved by lawyers. The subsequent influence of this on the integrity of the ACGIH process is unknown; still, unsuspecting workers currently exposed to trona, refractory ceramic fibers, and untold numbers of other compounds have no idea if or how their health was just influenced by these negotiated settlements.

***

Worker health and safety is under serious attack from all sides. OSHA's regulatory process is so complicated, costly and ineffective, and the political pressure so great, that good, new protective laws are essentially impossible. Furthermore, the agency can't work off directives and opinion letters (an admittedly undesirable alternative to begin with) because they too are scrutinized and attacked by industry and Congress. So, while OSHA holds the enormous responsibility for our nation's workplace safety and health, at the same time it is restricted from revising it's standards, issuing new ones and even writing guidelines. Meanwhile, reliance on consensus standards grows at the same time industry attacks them.

The collective amount of industry power and money spent fighting OSHA and lobbying Congress defy description in these few pages. Regardless of the particular health and safety issue, the debates are political and exclusive. They are not about health, and they are not aired on the evening news. Instead, they slither through well-funded industry websites, press releases and newsletters. For the most part, only lawyers, politicians, business leaders and technical people know about them. Often, the bottom line issue of damage—the alleged goal of reducing physical harm to workers—is not even discussed while cost, regulatory process and liability are analyzed and argued to death.

OSHA's efforts to protect worker welfare are no match against the wealth of the industries it is supposed to regulate. More horrifying is the possibility of organizations like ACGIH losing lawsuits or being barraged with more. There will be a dramatic change in America when private, non-profit professional societies can no longer speak their collective, scientific minds. Similar groups will also be silenced by the fear of expensive legal battles. If the wealth and power of industry succeed in encroaching on voluntary organizations like ACGIH, the fate of worker safety and health will be sealed. Then, even the most vigilant companies will have nowhere to turn.

Legalities, politics and money have overridden the human rights issue of worker health and safety. Worker health and safety is becoming nothing more than a business line item.

CHAPTER 7

Ergonomics

Death by Bureaucracy

Before she got carpal tunnel syndrome, Maddie typed 100 words per minute into the computer as she spoke with customers over the phone. She was valuable in her customer service job and had no problems until she began waking up with her hands fast asleep. Although she's had surgery on both wrists, she still says, "For the first few hours of every day, my elbows, forearms, wrists and fingers feel like they've been through the wringer. My forearms ache like I've been carrying around 100 pound suitcases for days."

When she realized she could no longer work, Maddie finally filed for workers compensation. She still can't work. "I cannot use my hands to write (even checks) or obviously to type. My hands are numb about 90 percent of the time which does not make for real finger dexterity, much less speed and accuracy."

"I am unable to open jars, take loads out of the wash, empty the dishwasher, make a bed, weed the garden, walk the dog, take out the garbage, cook dinner, turn on the electric toothbrush, do my hair, button a blouse, thread a needle, vacuum a room—all these things cause extreme pain in the arms when I extend my arms out. Trying to hold onto anything, grasp someone's hand...pain, pain, pain. I am so tired of the pain. I am never without it."

Because of the constant pain, Maddie makes excuses not to do things that most people take for granted—shopping, going out with friends, even just hanging out. During her few "periods of feeling okay" she seizes the moment to do the necessary things of life like run the vacuum. Plus, she admits "I try desperately not to talk about my pain when I'm with people. I lie and tell them I'm fine. My good friends know the truth; my significant other has been trained to carry all items for me when we go out and not to expect much participation from me as far as household projects."

Unable to drive her 5-speed coupe, Maddie elaborates on the effect carpal tunnel syndrome has had on her life. "I can't drive because the shifting kills my right arm. And with all the hydrocodeine I'm living on, I should not be driving anyway. Hydrocodeine makes you lose all sense of urgency, patience and alertness. That is not the way I would choose to be behind the wheel of a car. You wouldn't want me behind you."

In addition to her personal pain and job loss, Maddie sums up her situation by saying, "It has made a substantial impact on our social life and my interaction with others. My moods are usually dangerous. Why would I want to be around anyone when I feel so bad?"

***

Ergonomics is a millennial marketing buzzword. Companies tout "ergonomic design" on everything from keyboards to baby strollers to cookware. In the workplace, ergonomics is how tools, machines and workstations fit the individual workers and operators using them. A poor fit leaves the body in unnatural and awkward positions long enough to cause problems. A good fit, on the other hand, is comfortable, productive and safe. Ergonomics is basically the science of how people and their environment fit together.

The human body was not designed to do any one task 8 hours per day, 5 days per week, 50 weeks per year. Computer operators; cashiers and stockers; forklift and equipment operators; laboratory personnel; assemblers; and garbage collectors are all examples of workers routinely facing ergonomic hazards usually from constant, fast and repetitive movements. Maddie's carpal tunnel syndrome resulted from the excessive, unnatural demand placed on her wrists, hands and forearms from constant typing.

While someone working a jackhammer may face more obvious ergonomic hazards, a person making circuit boards who contracts their hand muscles all day to hold a small pair of pliers also risks ergonomic injury. Repetition, poor posture and forceful awkward movements can cause all sorts of ailments, such as muscle pulls, slipped discs, tendonitis; or the prevalent pinched nerve problem in the wrist called carpal tunnel syndrome. White-collar workers face ergonomic risks and so do manufacturing and construction workers. Ergonomics is non-discriminatory; it can affect anyone.

Ergonomics might not sound as important as electrical or heavy equipment safety, but in reality, poor ergonomics is the most common source of occupational injury and illness in the United States today. Every year, 600,000 work-related musculoskeletal disorders (MSDs) are severe enough to keep workers home. MSDs consume $1 of every $3 spent for workers' compensation. Total expenses associated with these injuries bring the costs up near $50 billion each year.[1] Since many work-related ergonomic ailments are denied or never reported, taxpayers and injured workers foot a large part of the bill.

Ergonomic ailments are well known. As far back as 1985, in response to a request from Congress, the Office of Technology Assessment prepared a report directly concluding, "Painful and sometimes incapacitating repetitive-motion disorders are associated with assembly-line work."[2] In July of 1997, NIOSH identified over 2,000 studies on work-related MSDs and reviewed over 600 of them in detail. NIOSH then published peer-reviewed results concluding, "A large body of credible epidemiologic research exists that shows a consistent relationship between MSDs and certain physical factors, especially at higher exposure levels.[3]

In 1998, a Congressionally mandated study by the National Academy of Sciences (NAS) clearly concluded: "There is a higher incidence of reported pain, injury, loss of work, and disability among individuals who are employed in occupations where there is a high level of exposure to physical loading than for those employed in occupations with lower levels of exposure. There is strong biological plausibility to the relationship between the incidence of musculoskeletal disorders and the causative exposure factors in high-exposure occupational settings. Research clearly demonstrates that specific interventions can reduce the reported rate of musculoskeletal disorders for workers who perform high-risk tasks. No known single intervention is universally effective. Successful interventions require attention to individual, organizational, and job characteristics, tailoring the corrective actions to those characteristics." Translated, the NAS conclusion means: poor ergonomics can cause injury and illness—use common sense and control the hazards.

Many companies realize this and have successfully controlled ergonomics for years. As early as 1989 and 1990, OSHA signed corporate-wide settlement agreements for ergonomic programs with Chrysler, General Motors and Ford Motor Company to control cumulative trauma disorders.

OSHA spent over a decade studying ergonomics, analyzing evidence, reviewing data, talking to stakeholders, and discussing ideas and options. And yet, despite the studies, the widespread suffering and almost unimaginable costs of ergonomic injuries and illnesses, OSHA has no ergonomics standard because the business community fiercely fought it every step of the way.

***

In 1996, Ed Hayden testified to the U.S. House of Representatives' Committee on Small Business. From the Milwaukee chapter, he testified on behalf of the Associated

General Contractors (AGC) of America, a powerful trade association of over 33,000 companies including 7,500 leading construction contracting firms. The same testimony was basically canned and repeated verbatim by Mike Lail, also on behalf of AGC, one year later at a Senate hearing on OSHA Reform.[4] Mr. Hayden said:

> In fact, there is no sound scientific data that proves musculoskeletal disorders (ergonomics injuries) reported by construction workers are work related. Despite the fact there is no sound scientific evidence for this regulation, OSHA stands ready to impose it on every company, regardless of size, in the construction industry. The compliance costs alone of the proposed ergonomics standard will be in the billions of dollars. Small contractors will have to hire outside help in order to comply with this standard. The end result of the proposed ergonomics standard will be higher construction costs, transferred onto consumers, and fewer job opportunities for construction workers. Until there is sound scientific proof that ergonomics injuries are caused by tasks performed at a construction site, OSHA should withdraw its proposed ergonomics standard.[5]

This one paragraph of testimony typifies the standard industry mantra against OSHA's ergonomic standard; it illustrates how industry dehumanizes a health discussion into one of economics and science. The canned argument against the OSHA ergonomics standard, like many arguments against OSHA, relied on the following staples:

1. Attack the science to delay, delay, delay.

2. Charge OSHA as irrational in even attempting to create one standard for all workplaces.

3. Defend industry's right to "freedom from regulation" with the threat of job losses and small business bankruptcies.

4. Never acknowledge the injuries, illnesses and suffering.

The concern isn't, "Has the exposure been determined NOT

to cause harm?" Instead, error is made on the side of protecting industry's money instead of protecting worker health and safety. Why is the money necessary to implement precautions of greater value than the health of the employee that would be protected? Or even the worker that might be protected? If there is legitimate scientific doubt, why not err on the side of worker health in the meanwhile?

Imagine if drugs were prescribed before they were proven safe, or if medical procedures were performed before they were sufficiently researched. When consumers can sue manufacturers for faulty products, those products tend to be researched and made safe before they hit the marketplace. Not so in the case of worker safety and health, where the worker's compensation system shields employers from injury and illness lawsuits. Occupational health and safety is the only arena where people are not only allowed to face hazards that pose known or uncertain health risks, they are expected to.

***

The Opposition

A major foe of OSHA's ergonomic standard is the National Association of Manufacturers (NAM)—the nation's largest, broad-based industrial trade group with membership including more than 14,000 companies and subsidiaries and 350 member associations, from every state.

NAM does not try to hide its influence. They write letters to Congressional leaders, like the one sent on August 2, 1999 to House Representative William Goodling which read in part, "On behalf of our member companies, we urge you to support H.R. 987, "The Workplace Preservation Act. This bipartisan legislation is simple: It would prevent OSHA from moving ahead with an ergonomics regulation until a comprehensive review of all medical studies related to MSDs is completed by the NAS." NAM was not satisfied with the findings of the first

NAS study, which already affirmed the ergonomic cause and effect relationship, and wanted OSHA to wait for a second NAS study.[6] While NAM reiterated the industry mantra that OSHA should wait for 18-24 months until a new, presumably 'sounder' study could take place, the letter made no mention of the 1.2 million MSDs that would occur in the meanwhile.

NAM closed its letter to Representative Goodling by saying, "H.R. 987 will be considered for designation as a Key Manufacturing Vote in the NAM's Voting Record for the 106th Congress. We hope you will support this bill, which is so critical to the NAM and the employer community." In other words, NAM will tell its members to support Goodling based on his vote, a serious threat to voter-dependent and campaign-contribution-dependent politicians.

Beginning as an offshoot from the NAM subcommittee on OSHA policy,[7] the National Coalition on Ergonomics (NCE) is a monstrous alliance representing more than 300 associations and businesses across every sector of industry in the United States. The money and influence wielded by this association created for and dedicated solely to fighting the promulgation of an OSHA ergonomics standard is enormous.

Most NCE supporting organizations listed below are associations of employers, each representing tens, hundreds or even thousands of employers.

NCE Website "Who We Are: Endorsement List"
Academy of General Dentistry
American Ambulance Association
American Bakers Association
American Feed Industry Association
American Foundrymen's Society
American Hardware Manufacturers Association
American Hotel & Motel Association
American Iron and Steel Institute

American Small Businesses Association
   American Staffing Association
   American Trucking Associations
   Associated Builders and Contractors
Associated General Contractors of America
Can Manufacturers Institute
Center for Office Technology
City of Rochester Solid Waste Management Division
Corn Refiners Association, Inc.
Food Distributors International
Food Marketing Institute
   Four Corners Distributing
General Building Contractors (New York State Chapter of
   Associated General Contractors of America)
Gas Appliance Manufacturers Association
Gold Cities Beverage
Golden Eagle Distributing
Gypsum Association
Hardwood, Plywood and Veneer Association
Institute for Interconnecting and Packaging of Electronic
   Circuits
Institute of Makers of Explosives
Institute of Shortening and Edible Oils
International Mass Retail Association
International Warehouse Logistics Association
M-C Industries, Inc.
Morrey Distributing Co.
National Association of Convenience Stores
National Association of Home Builders
National Association of Manufacturers
National Association of the Remodeling Industry
National Beer Wholesalers Association
National Federation of Independent Business
National Grocers Association

National Roofing Contractors Association
National Soft Drink Association
National Utility Contractors Association
New Jersey Business & Industry Association
North American Die Casting Association
Painting and Decorating Contractors of America
Petitpren Inc.
Precision Metalforming Association
Snack Food Association
Society of American Florists
Talk O'Texas Brands, Inc.
Textile Rental Services Association of America
Thorpe Distributing Company
Uniform and Textile Service Association
United States Chamber of Commerce
Watkins Distributing
... and more than 250 organizations nationwide.

Named like an impartial, educational group, the NCE maintains their own website and provides "information" on ergonomics. The front page of the website blares, "Should businesses become laboratories for costly, unscientific government regulations? That's exactly the result under the ergonomic regulation just promulgated by OSHA. This regulation forces experimental, unproven and financially ruinous requirements on virtually every private employer in the nation (with the exception of specified industries that are not yet covered.) It forces employers to teach employees the scientifically invalid and false assumptions underlying the rule as if they were truths. Yet, despite the billions of dollars it will cost, this ergonomic regulation will not assure the prevention of a single injury." The NCE website and this extreme, sensationalized statement shows just how far an attack on science can be taken.

The NCE home page, for example, bluntly states, "We are

dedicated to a full debate concerning ergonomics — the practice of fitting workplaces to workers." Why is the NCE dedicated to a debate rather than to a resolution? Because an endless debate delays the standard indefinitely, and a delay is the same as a win.

Like a textbook on how to delay OSHA regulations, the NCE website employs the other commonly used staples, including invoking emotion with the defense that the regulation will cost jobs. A fact sheet section titled "A High Price to Pay for No Assurance of Prevention" is intended to solicit a knee jerk response to the obvious stupidity of a regulation that would cost money and produce no results. It said:

> Who gets hit the hardest when such a far-reaching and costly regulation is imposed? Those who can least afford it — small businesses that would be forced to comply with the regulation, and consumers who would pay higher prices for goods and services. When businesses are forced to spend billions complying with government regulations, many would be forced to close shop, contract with foreign suppliers, or automate jobs, all of which would result in laying off employees. We must create jobs, not eliminate them.[8]

At the same time these industries collectively and publicly deny the validity of the science behind the ergonomic standard, many of the same voluntarily run their own ergonomics programs. Their programs are not based on whim and fancy, but on the best available science—the very science the NCE claims is nonexistent. For years companies have run ergonomic programs without "being forced to close shop or automate jobs and lay off employees."

Just one NCE backer is the Food Marketing Institute, representing 1,500 members responsible for three-quarters of all national grocery store sales. Since 1992, the Food Marketing Institute offered its members a manual to provide "various suggestions for modifying checkstand designs and cashier work activities that can help decrease ergonomic stressors for cashiers, while maintaining and even improving cashier effectiveness and productivity."[9] In 1995, a video guide for distribution supervisors was provided to educate "order selectors about proper body movements when selecting merchandise; proper pallet handling; and safe selecting techniques, from developing a plan for selecting an order to delivering a stable load of merchandise to the dock."[10] And in 1996, the Food Marketing Institute provided a report on "an overview of scientific research conducted at The Ohio State University Biodynamics Laboratory on checkstands and scanning equipment."[11] That is a strange report for an organization supporting the "no sound science" claim.

In 1999, the then-head of OSHA, Charles Jeffress, spoke to The National Coalition on Ergonomics and said, "Individually many of the 200 companies that publicly support the coalition's effort to discredit and delay an ergonomics standard have also established ergonomics programs. I challenge those corporations to preach what they practice. I urge you, as spokesmen and spokeswomen for these corporations to understand that people see you as saying one thing and doing another. You cry "wolf" about ergonomics, while at the same time investing in ergonomics programs to protect your employees. Have you no shame? Do you not care about the reputation for misrepresentation that you are creating for your corporations?"[12]

Contrary to industry claims, ergonomic programs have been shown to be a good thing. As recently as August 1997 and at the request of Congress, five companies voluntarily implementing ergonomics programs were studied. They included: American Express Financial Advisors, Inc.—5,300 staff; AMP Incorporated—300 staff; Navistar International Transportation Corporation—4,000 staff; Sisters of Charity Health System—780 staff; and Texas Instruments—2,800 staff. The report stated:

Controls did not typically require significant investment or resources and did not drastically change the job or operation. Officials at all the facilities we visited believed their ergonomics programs yielded benefits, including reductions in workers' compensation costs associated with MSDs....Facility officials also reported improved worker morale, productivity, and product quality....[13]

Private sector employers spend about $60 billion annually on workers' compensation costs associated with injuries and illnesses experienced by their employees.[14] With so much money at stake, it would seem that industry would want an OSHA ergonomic standard. One reason they don't is the gray areas.

Industry only wants to address the black and white issues, those that clearly cost them money. But there are gray areas where employee pain and discomfort come into play. While many companies voluntarily institute ergonomics programs to curb their costs, OSHA's endpoint is employee health and well-being.

OSHA seeks to eliminate pain and suffering, improve comfort and reduce long term illnesses that may not even be attributable to any one employer. If an employer is not on the financial hook for an injury or illness, why spend money on its prevention? Because of an OSHA standard. That's one reason why industry fights it.

Acknowledging the gray areas, OSHA expressed its ergonomic intentions to the NCE. "One size does not fit all. That is why OSHA has decided on the program approach. That's also why no one will ever be able to say that X number of repetitions or lifting X pounds will result in injury or conversely that Y number of repetitions or Y pounds will definitely NOT result in injury for anyone, any time, anywhere. However, many employers have proven that establishing a systematic program to address such issues as repetition, excessive force, awkward postures and heavy lifting, results in fewer injuries to workers."[15]

Not good enough, said industry. "Any ergonomics regulation must be supported by sound science," said Ed Gilroy, co-chair of the NCE. "Right now there is no consensus in the medical and scientific communities on fundamental questions about ergonomics. For example: How many repetitions result in injury? How heavy a lift is too heavy? What is an awkward position? Employers need these answers to know what OSHA's regulation would require."[16]

A Popular Ploy

Industry tends to treat occupational health and safety issues like it treats environmental issues. There never is frank debate about science, just regurgitated rhetoric sufficient to build an obscuring smokescreen. The result is that inaction becomes action, a choice to continue exposing people to recognized hazards. Over and over again, this political ploy works.

In 2000, Jack Doyle published "Taken for a Ride: Detroit's Big Three and the Politics of Pollution." In the introduction to his exhaustive chronology, Doyle describes how the car manufacturing industry teamed together to avoid government regulation of auto pollution. He wrote, "Time and time again in the 1950's, 1960's, 1970's, 1980's and through the 1990's, the automakers said, "We don't have the technology." "it's impossible," "we don't have the money," "we don't have the engineers," "we're at a competitive disadvantage," "it will be too disruptive," "it will make cars unsafe," etc. Yet this is an industry that once never shrank from technological challenge, an industry filled with capability and dynamic leaders, CEO's of action and "can do" engineers ready to tackle any problem."[17]

The tactic of claiming inadequate science was so successful for the tobacco industry that they dodged responsibility for decades by arguing that smoking had never been proven to cause cancer. Although their credibility waned, they stuck to this argument to the end. Similar to the argument over ergonomics, denials made by the tobacco and automotive industry work because they keep attention on the scientific and legal details, rather than on the underlying massive health problem. The voices of the sufferers are swept away in the flow of industry money and lawyers.

On April 19, 2001, The Wall Street Journal ran a front page article titled *Dangerous Waters—All Agree Arsenic Kills; The Question Is How Much It Takes To Do So*. It began:

After declaring that arsenic in drinking water causes cancer, it took the EPA 17 years, and six intense weeks at the tail end of the Clinton administration, to order sharp reductions of the naturally occurring carcinogen in America's water supply.

It took the Bush administration 58 days to scrap the new rule. The Wall Street Journal noted:

> "At the very last minute, my predecessor made a decision" to lower arsenic standards, said President George W. Bush last month. "We pulled back his decision, so that we can make a decision based upon sound science."
>
> In fact, few government decisions could have been more thoroughly researched, over so many years, than the EPA's move to slash the allowable content of arsenic in drinking water by 80%. The beefed-up standard, to 10 parts per billion from 50 ppb, was first proposed by the U.S. Public Health Service back in 1962.[18]

Approximately 15 million Americans drink water impacted by this ruling. The usually conservative Wall Street Journal quoted Richard Wilson, a Harvard University physics professor and former department chair who studies health risks as saying, "We know arsenic is carcinogenic in people—not just laboratory animals—at exposure levels that aren't much higher than the current U.S. standard. The science is unequivocal."[19]

The paper then reported, "Not to everyone. Since 1990, consultants working for corporations that could face billions of dollars in cleanup costs under a lower arsenic standard have cast doubts on the science. For ammunition, they funded studies, then shelved results they didn't like."[20]

Regardless of the health standard, industry's no sound science argument creates a need for absolute proof and places the burden for that proof on the government agency assigned to regulate the issue. In all cases, the delays cost people their health.

***

Congress—Hardly the Innocent Bystander

Despite the facts, industry was winning the ergonomic argument in Congress. Twice, Congress exerted its influence to the detriment of worker health and safety by literally prohibiting OSHA from proposing an ergonomics standard or even guidelines by adding a stipulation (called an appropriations rider) in the 1995 OSHA budget and again in 1996.[21] For a third time, in 1998, Congress intentionally impeded passage of an ergonomics standard with a restriction prohibiting OSHA from issuing a proposed or final ergonomics standard during the year, but they gave approval for OSHA to develop such a proposal in the meantime.[22] Tagging appropriations riders onto the budget is one of the ways Congress interferes with the established OSHA regulatory process, places special interests first, and undermines not only the science of occupational health and safety but also the very intent of the OSH Act.

The OSH Act states how OSHA is supposed to promulgate standards. Congressional appropriations riders roadblock this critical and sometimes lifesaving OSHA obligation. The Act reads:

...Development of standards under this subsection shall be based upon research, demonstrations, experiments, and such other information as may be appropriate. In addition to the attainment of the highest degree of health and safety protection for the employee, other considerations shall be the latest available scientific data in the field, the feasibility of the standards, and experience gained under this and other health and safety laws. Whenever practicable, the standard promulgated shall be expressed in terms of objective criteria and of the performance desired.[23]

Although OSHA's mandate says nothing about cost, that seems to be what Congress was basing its decisions on. Ironically, it was Congress that pushed for the second NAS study on ergonomics to be sure employers were not rushed into paying for compliance. This stuck taxpayers with an additional $890,000 after already spending $490,000 on the first NAS study. Even worse, workers paid with their health and financial security as they incurred more than 600,000 ergonomic illnesses and injuries each additional year.

None of the 1.38 million dollars spent on the NAS studies should have been spent since NIOSH and OSHA had already evaluated and prepared recommendations on ergonomics. Taxpayers fund both these agencies, plus they paid for studies done by the Office of Technology Assessment and the General Accounting Office, all concluding the same thing.

***

No, ergonomics is not an exact science. That's because we're dealing with individuals, not robots. Apply the basic principles and adjust as needed. There's some trial and error involved. But it's not rocket science either.

—Charles Jeffress, speech to The National Coalition on Ergonomics, April 29, 1999

"Sound scientific evidence" and "sufficient scientific evidence" sounds like a bottom line, an achievable end, an absolute, black and white answer. But that is exactly the flaw in the argument, the assumption that there ever will be "sound" or "sufficient" scientific evidence. The "soundness" of most science—including the science of occupational health and safety—can always be argued because "soundness" is ultimately subjective. Ultimately, the "soundness" and "sufficiency" of science becomes reasonable judgment—a question of when enough is enough.

The scientific method is the backbone of discovery. First, someone forms a theory (a hypothesis) and then studies are done to challenge it. If the studies show the results predicted by the hypothesis, that does not mean the hypothesis is true. It only means that it might be true because some unrecognized factor(s) might be involved. The more studies that show the predicted results, the stronger the hypothesis appears and the greater the probability that it is true. The more tests confirming the hypothesis, the more believable it becomes.

A theory that has not been disproven is not necessarily true—only that it is likely to be true. How likely depends on the type and number of challenges made against the hypothesis. No matter how technologically advanced we become, this fundamental rule of science—the scientific method—always applies. Since the days when fire was first discovered, the scientific method remains a fundamental building block of scientific discovery.

As a nation, however, we have become accustomed to health and science in terms of precise numbers and black and white answers. We ask, "Is this water safe to drink?" "To swim in?" "Is this diet healthy?" "How safe is this car?" "Is this toy non-toxic?" While these are reasonable questions asked by responsible people, truthful answers to these types of questions are not "yes" or "no" but are more accurately "probably" and "probably not."

Intentionally or unintentionally, industry and the media foster this misunderstanding about the scientific method and the very real limits of science. Imagine a drug commercial touting that their newest drug advance is "probably safe" for you to take?" Or a press release announcing that researchers are "reasonably confident" that a new vaccine won't cause long term side effects to your helpless and heretofore healthy infant? How about a car warranty promising short drivers "an unlikely risk of serious and remote risk of life threatening injury" from air bag deployment?

Today's news media foster this misunderstanding partly because they need to tell stories in a quick, entertaining way. Newspapers struggling to compete with television, glossy magazines and the Internet cannot afford to bore readers with the dry details and limitations of scientific discoveries. Television news shows have resident doctors translating the latest scientific discoveries into twenty-second soundbites; one local news show in Central Pennsylvania regularly features a "medical minute" on new developments and studies.

Adding to the confusion is the fact that limits of all kinds are common: we follow "safe" diet recommendations; drugs are "proven safe and effective;" "safe" speed limits are enforced; above a certain blood alcohol content is drunk; and, residual pesticide levels on food are deemed "safe for human consumption." Our blood cholesterol levels are no longer just high or low but also good or bad. In this information age, the general public expects technology and experts in white lab coats to provide definitive answers. We like it and want it that way.

But the pursuit of knowledge is just that—a pursuit. Researchers will never collectively push back from their desks one day and announce, "Well, we're done." Science and technology will continue to advance and what is considered safe or unsafe today may or may not be tomorrow.

In the case of ergonomics, studies and real world injuries strongly support the "hypothesis" that poor "fit" results in numerous types and degrees of injury and illness. Although never disproven, this hypothesis has not been proven to be true in the same way the speed of light has been proven true. And while studies and tests have repetitively confirmed ergonomic cause and effect relationships well beyond the point of common sense, they cannot predict with absolute scientific certainty that, for example, when Joe Rodgers swings down from his tractor trailer for the 2,345 time, he is going to tear his left rotator cuff.

The more studies, the more believable the hypothesis. This fundamental law of science—the scientific method—is no reason to delay advances in worker safety and health any more than it should delay progress in aerospace, engineering or medicine. At some point, the folks in white lab coats finish enough studies, build in a margin of safety for good measure, and the world moves on with a new drug, a spaceship built for Mars or a medical device like the ultrasound. The line has to be drawn somewhere.

While science is not and will not ever be perfect, that fact does not warrant inaction or indefinite study in any field, especially in occupational health where the alternative is injury and illness. More studies can always be done because the numbers and combinations of hazards, exposures and confounding factors are infinite.

In his 1996 testimony to the U.S. House of Representatives Committee on Small Business, Ed Hayden of the AGC said,

> The imposition of an ergonomics standard on the construction industry does not make sense. Simply put, the human body develops more aches and pains as it ages. Construction craftsmen are known to work many hours outside their 9-5 jobs, plying their crafts to earn extra income. Many construction workers also lead an active lifestyle outside the workplace. An ergonomic standard would

> place the responsibility for wear and tear to the
> human body caused by these activities and the
> aging process solely on the employer. There's no
> recognition by OSHA that safe practices put in
> place by employers make the workplace safer than
> the activity the employee participates in outside of
> his workplace.[24]

Granted, sometimes exposures on the job are affected by outside factors. Occupational asthma, for example, may be affected by environmental factors like high ozone. Conversely, people with non-occupational asthma conditions may become chemically sensitized from an exposure on the job. Neither example, however, excuses the employer from their responsibility to provide safe and healthful workplaces or from taking steps to remove or reduce hazardous exposures. Valid logic does not lead to the conclusion that OSHA should waive a protective regulation simply because exposures *may* occur both on and off the job.

Bill was employed by the same steel tube manufacturer for 43 years. "Basically, I hung steel tubing on hooks. The steel tubes are long and heavy, and you lift three or four at a time. I spent 39 years on the paint line, loading and unloading tubes. Workers there are either loaders, operators or unloaders."

In 1996, Bill had such pain in his back that he could hardly walk from the car to his house. An MRI showed a bulged disk. Electrical diagnostic tests on his arms showed carpal tunnel syndrome in both. Bill filed for workers compensation for a repetitive motion injury. In 1966, he had used his own insurance to pay for surgery to repair a work-related herniated disk.

Bill is 62 years old, and says he has arthritis and degenerated disks. Are his back problems from age? From riding his lawn mower one hour each weekend? Is his carpal tunnel syndrome from throwing a ball to his grandchild?

"C'mon." says Bill. "It's from yanking and hanging heavy steel tubing all my life."

***

Bold Opposition

In April of 2000 I sat with 50 or so other industrial hygiene and safety professionals in a two day conference on ergonomics. A Certified Professional Ergonomist taught us how force, repetition and posture affect worker comfort, productivity and safety. Our manual included tables and diagrams showing optimum reach distances, work heights, rotation angles and viewing ranges. It said things like, "For operators working in a standing position, the width of control placement should not exceed 42 inches. Vertical placement of controls should be between 40 inches and 50 inches above the standing surface."[25] We learned, for example, the maximum recommended control activation forces—the physical effort required to push/pull buttons, toggles, cranks, pedals and trigger. We got information on biomechanics; for instance, the force to safely operate and control power and manual hand tools should be less than six pounds total force per hand.[26] In other words, we were taught the current science of ergonomics.

David Sarvadi is both a Certified Industrial Hygienist (CIH) and a lawyer. On the second day of our conference on state-of-the-art ergonomics, he spoke to us on behalf of the NCE about the proposed OSHA ergonomic standard.[27] After presenting the standard "no sound science" rhetoric, a frustrated attendee refuted it saying that responsible companies already address ergonomics; it is the irresponsible ones that require a standard—a law forcing them to address it. David Sarvadi responded, "Do you gain a competitive advantage by having an ergonomics program?" When the startled woman said yes, he replied, "Then why do you want an ergonomics standard so other companies gain that same advantage?"

Because people are getting hurt and there is incredible, needless suffering.

Because we have the ability to do something.

Because health and welfare is also of value.

Moments later, another woman said, "I hear you taking the standard apart line by line with criticisms, but what kinds of proactive, positive things has your organization done?" The NCE lawyer immediately said, "It's not our job to come up with a standard. It is not our job to define hazard."

Those crying about the supposed lack of ergonomic science are not offering any alternatives because their single goal is to stop or slow OSHA law as much as possible for as long as possible. This could not be more apparent than in this demonstration by an NCE lawyer, who is also a CIH, unashamedly standing in front of a class of career health and safety professionals that just sat through an ergonomic course, and with a straight face suggest (1) that the science is inadequate and (2) that we consider how our employers' ergonomic programs give our companies a competitive advantage. Even these two points conflict: if he agrees that ergonomic programs offer a competitive advantage, how can he still argue that there is inadequate science?

That same lawyer was quoted after the NCE teamed with the equally powerful National Association of Manufacturers and others to sue OSHA to stop the final OSHA ergonomics standard. Sarvadi said of the lawsuit, "Who knows what will happen. From a lawyer's perspective, there is so much juicy material here that it's hard to predict. There is the controversy with the state of the science behind ergonomics, we have a significant public relations component, Congress is involved, and the election outcome isn't resolved."[28] Meanwhile, the NCE website showed a cartoon of a sweating, blind-folded business person with a bulls-eye target on his head. Worker well-being could not have degraded farther from the discussion.

***

After decades of research, OSHA finally issued a proposed ergonomics standard on November 15, 1999. Lawsuits were immediately filed.

On January 24, 2001, the Washington Post printed an op/ed article written by Thomas J. Donohue, the President and CEO of the U.S. Chamber of Commerce. Titled, "Mother of Regulations: The Death of Common Sense in the Workplace," it started, "Last week, the most costly, burdensome, and far-reaching government regulation in U.S. history took effect, marking a dangerous new government intrusion into the private-sector workplace and the lives of honest, hardworking Americans."

In March, 2001, Congress used the Congressional Review Act for the first time to overturn OSHA's final ergonomic standard. President George W. Bush signed it, rendering OSHA's final ergonomic standard—a standard ten years in the making—null and void. As a result, OSHA is literally banned from issuing any "substantially similar" standard without an act of Congress.

President George W. Bush commented, "There needs to be a balance between and an understanding of the costs and benefits associated with Federal regulations. In this instance, though, in exchange for uncertain benefits, the ergonomics rule would have cost both large and small employers billions of dollars and presented employers with overwhelming compliance challenges. Also, the rule would have applied a bureaucratic one-size-fits-all solution to a broad range of employers and workers—not good government at work."[29]

Congressional Minority Leader Dick Gephardt was quoted at a news conference saying, "I have not in my entire time in Congress seen such an awful example of rushing to the floor just a few months after an election, and trying to get through special-interest legislation [against the workplace ergonomics rule] that rolls over all the studies, all the logic, all the results that have come from all the work that's been done in both Democratic and Republican administrations."[30]

John Sweeney, President of the AFL-CIO said, "The voices of injured workers were not heard in the halls of Congress. They were drowned out by the predatory demands of corporate greed."[31]

***

The scientific literature shows that certain work factors cause musculoskeletal disorders and that musculoskeletal disorders are a major problem leading to adverse health and economic consequences. Through effective programs the pain and disability of musculoskeletal disorders can be reduced, workers' compensation costs can be cut, and productivity and employee satisfaction can be improved. We can take these steps now—as we have done with other occupational health problems—at the same time we continue to do research and become smarter about the causes and solutions of these problems. We know quite a bit—we have more to learn. In science as in life, knowledge may be imperfect, but to deny what we do know about these complex problems is to deny the American worker the benefits of that knowledge.

—Linda Rosenstock, Director of NIOSH,
May 21, 1997.
Testimony to the Subcommittee
on Workforce Protection.

History has proven that, on the whole, industry does not voluntarily manage safety and health to the uniform degree desired by society. Especially in the area of occupational health and safety where workers compensation protects employers from lawsuits, there must be regulations and government enforcement to hold all employers equally accountable. As a nation, we cannot rely on corporate values alone.

Between the lines of well rehearsed, well-dressed and anonymous lawyer-speak is the individual savagery of corporate leaders and politicians choosing money over people's health. Hiding behind large industry associations, lobbyists, public relations firms and lawyers are well-paid business leaders putting their bottom line first. Whether they admit it or not, the issue is profit versus health. The same people making the bottom line possible are the ones sacrificed.

CHAPTER 8

OSHA—Part of the Problem or Part of the Solution?

Its not easy being an OSHA Compliance Officer. Imagine knocking on the door of a business for an unannounced inspection. No one is happy to see you. You may even enter a place that threatens your own health and safety.

As an OSHA Compliance Officer, you are expected to be an expert on volumes of regulations, procedures, chemicals and equipment. You need the personal skills to deal with employers who mistrust you, employees that fear you, and lawyers from both OSHA and industry that will scrutinize your work. In addition, you earn less than your peers in industry and you receive less training and recognition. Still, you bear enormous influence on the welfare of hundreds, maybe thousands, of workers.

One of the most critical facts to know about OSHA is that the agency is equipped with less than 2,200 inspectors for over 7 million workplaces. With current funding and staffing, OSHA's assignment to "assure safe and healthful working conditions for working men and women"[1] is humanly impossible. Add that fact to the public's lack of awareness and support, throw in chronic Congressional and industry belittling and the nation has a recipe for the ineffective OSHA now in place.

Beyond the obvious problems at OSHA is a lesser known, seedy underside: its indefensible protection of the very corporations responsible for maiming and sickening workers. In order to create a healthy OSHA, one that fights consistently and fairly for worker welfare, exposing this aspect of the agency is essential to show the changes needed to make a meaningful dent in the mountain of illnesses and injuries plaguing our nation.

The Legacy of Patrick Hayes

Ron Hayes knows OSHA. Since his 19-year-old son, Patrick, was killed in a Florida grain silo in 1993, Ron has become expert on the agency.

Patrick's employer sent him into the top of a silo to "walk the corn"—a deadly practice barred by the OSHA grain-handling standard. Earning $5 an hour, Patrick's task that day was to manually push corn from the sides of the silo, where it piles up, into the middle. Unprotected, Patrick walked on top of 35 feet of corn while an auger rotated dangerously beneath the piled feedstock.

When an air pocket collapsed below, there was nothing to prevent Patrick from sinking like someone caught in quicksand. He suffocated under tons of corn. One of Ron's most painful memories is identifying his son's body in the morgue; he can still see Patrick's face contorted in pain, tears streaked through the corn dust on his face.

Mobilized by grief, Ron investigated his son's employer, Showell Farms. During the previous 18 years, he found they were inspected 25 times by OSHA and cited for more than 80 violations. The OSHA compliance officer assigned to investigate Patrick's death wrote up Showell Farms for five alleged willful violations and one serious violation. The proposed penalty totaled $530,000.

Ron would later learn from the local television news that OSHA dropped the penalty to $30,000 and downgraded the citation from willful (meaning the employer was plainly indifferent to or intentionally violated the OSHA Act) to serious (meaning the employer did not recognize a hazard that could cause death or serious physical harm). This downgrade put the owners and operators of Showell Farms beyond the reach of criminal prosecution, a short-circuit of justice that pains Ron and his family to this day.

Outraged and devastated, Ron tried to get information, but

all he could obtain was a couple of pages of the police report. He waited six months for a response from OSHA, and even had to fight for a copy of the autopsy report from the coroner's office. This lack of information and disrespect, Ron says, made the already unbearable ordeal that much worse.

Finally, Ron filed multiple written requests under the Freedom of Information Act (FOIA) for information on Patrick's case. Frustrated from waiting for a response, Ron's wife re-wrote the original typed FOIA request by hand on plain paper. They signed it "Jake McLean," after their friend's dog, and mailed it in. One day after receiving Jake's request, OSHA mailed a dog the information it would not mail to Ron.

Still, Ron refused to go away. Instead, he committed himself to making workplaces safer and helping families through similar horror stories. He quit his comfortable job as an x-ray technician and along with his wife, founded the non-profit Families In Grief Hold Together (The FIGHT Project). The FIGHT Project has helped over 450 families in all 50 states cope with the tragedy of a workplace fatality, and they have never charged a single penny for their services. Following Patrick's senseless death and the cruel treatment his family received afterwards, Ron says of his life's mission, "Pat's gone but maybe I can save someone else's kid. I can definitely help the families suffering through this nightmare."

While he wholeheartedly supports OSHA's mission, Ron says "The agency has not been consistent and they have ruined the system. They've violated their own policies and procedures, and now they can't stand behind them. They have lost compassion and respect." With resignation, he concedes, "For the worker, OSHA is shot."

He explains, "Compliance Officers within OSHA lose respect for the organization, as do workers when they finally call OSHA to come protect them. Most people dealing with OSHA eventually learn that you cannot count on the organization, but they all start out believing that OSHA can and will help."

Many workers interviewed for this book did call their local OSHA offices to voice concern about their workplaces, and as Ron observed with his own situation and those of the families he helps, they felt let down by OSHA. Not one was satisfied with OSHA's response, and after reviewing many of their cases, their concerns proved legitimate.

OSHA's own rulebook—the Field Reference Inspection Manual (FIRM)—explains, for example, how a person wishing to make a formal complaint can do so. All they have to do is call the local OSHA office, complete a form over the phone with an OSHA representative and sign it when they receive a copy in the mail. Or, the caller can write a letter to OSHA with the requisite information, and an OSHA officer can complete the form and begin an investigation.[2]

But when one worker called in an exposure complaint, she was told she would have to physically travel to the OSHA office to sign the complaint. She never did because she could not afford a day off to make the trip. Another worker, an x-ray technician suspecting her neurological problems were work-related, called OSHA when she discovered an x-ray processor ventilation tube discharging into the drop-ceiling space above her office. She said, "First, OSHA told me I should call the EPA. Then, they told me I needed other people in the office to sign a complaint. I couldn't because I was the only one sitting in the room for six hours with the x-ray processor, and no one else was sick." Of course, neither worker was familiar with correct OSHA procedure and none even suspected that they should challenge what they were told. This wrongdoing, says Ron, is the consequence of OSHA's lost compassion for those it is supposed to protect.

Complaints resulting in OSHA inspections also left dissatisfied workers. Explaining OSHA's policy on advance notice of inspections, the FIRM reads: "The OSHA Act regulates many conditions, which are subject to speedy alteration and disguise by employers. To forestall such changes in worksite conditions, the Act, in Section (8)(a), prohibits unauthorized advance notice." The FIRM explains further, "There may be occasions when advance notice is necessary to conduct an effective investigation. These occasions are narrow exceptions to the statutory prohibition against advance notice."[3] In other words, with very few exceptions, OSHA is not supposed to tell employers when they will be knocking on the front door.

Several chemically exposed workers, however, reported that OSHA arrived unannounced to their workplaces only to tell the employers when they would return to perform air monitoring. While some questioning of the employer is appropriate to understand operations, making specific arrangements for air sampling gives advance notice and thwarts the purpose. A 24-year veteran of a large mid-west printing company revealed, "OSHA came back three weeks later to do air sampling, and the boss knew they were coming. So, to reduce the solvent vapors, they ran half water through the system, opened every door, and turned on every air handler and air conditioner."

The worker, who suffers severe neurological damage from solvent exposure, continued, "The union representative accompanying the compliance officer on the day of the sampling heard workers tell him that the sampling was a joke and that results would be low. The compliance officer actually said that other workers told him that already, yet he kept sampling. He never did return unannounced to sample, and he could have because we printed every day. It was utterly ridiculous. OSHA was no help at all."

Technically, OSHA is restricted only from giving advance notice of the initial visit. Common sense, however, dictates that the entire inspection should be un-announced, not just the opening day. This too, explains Ron, is evidence of how OSHA does not care enough to do its best.

This observation resounded loudly throughout many worker interviews. A Pennsylvania nurse suffering health effects from gluteraldehyde exposure spoke of the time OSHA came in to sample the air on New Year's Eve Day. "People don't choose holidays for elective surgery," she said. "OSHA knew we were not sterilizing the normal number of surgical items." Not surprisingly, OSHA found low contaminant levels.

A mid-western worker called OSHA after a methylene chloride release sent him and several of his co-workers to a medical clinic. OSHA came in and sampled the air after the release dissipated. Although the employer took no air samples during the release, they were not fined for a lack of exposure monitoring; instead, OSHA cited them for an earlier occasion when they surreptitiously took air samples at night and kept the results from the workers. No penalty was given, however, with the citation.

Since exposure records are like medical records, OSHA regulation gives employees a legal right to them. The still-sick employee, however, has been unable to get even copies of the nighttime air sampling results from his employer. He continues to suffer neurological disorders and persistent headaches, but is unable to bring his own exposure records to the physicians trying to diagnose his condition. He says, "OSHA was no help at all."

According to the OSHA methylene chloride standard, employers are supposed to perform initial, *representative* exposure monitoring when introducing MC to a workplace. They are also required to provide affected employees or their representatives an opportunity to observe any monitoring of employee exposure to methylene chloride conducted in accordance with the standard. In this case, OSHA failed to cite and enforce these requirements.

In fact, the OSHA Area Director wrote a letter to the employer stating "No emergency response plan was developed to address a potential release or spill of methylene chloride. Since no OSHA standard applies and it is not considered appropriate at this time to invoke Section 5(a)(1), the general duty clause of the Occupational Safety and Health Act, no citation will be issued for these hazards." The letter recommended that the employer voluntarily prepare written procedures for a spill.

But the methylene chloride standard states, "The employer shall implement procedures to detect leaks of MC in the workplace. In work areas where spills may occur, the employer shall make provisions to contain any spills and to safely dispose of any MC-contaminated waste materials."[4] There *was* a violation of the standard, and yet the employer was not cited.

"The saddest part of it all" says Ron, "is that people believe in OSHA until they discover that OSHA also lacks compassion and respect. They see the response from their complaint, the negotiated penalty amounts, and they learn they can't count on OSHA either."

***

Unclassified Violations: U Stands for Ugly

> "Crouse-Hinds, a Division of Cooper Industries, Inc. in Syracuse, NY has agreed to pay a $350,000 penalty and to hire a consultant to monitor its progress in correcting health and safety hazards, following a Jan. 26, 1999 fatal accident at the company's Wolf Street facility."
>
> —OSHA Region 2 Press Release,
> July 26, 1999.

The image of a tough OSHA is enforced by OSHA's press releases touting large penalties. Big fines are supposed to show how hard OSHA is on employers that disregard worker health and safety. OSHA does not, however, issue press releases explaining how citations are reclassified and penalties negotiated. Indeed, not many people realize that OSHA penalties and citations *are* negotiable—not negotiable between OSHA and the injured or ill worker or the families of deceased workers but between the violating employer and OSHA.

Since its inception, OSHA had just four violations: willful, serious, repeat, and other-than-serious. In addition, a de minimis citation was issued when a violation was minor and not worthy of a penalty, such as using an incorrect warning color, and a failure-to-abate violation was issued when employers failed to comply with previous citations. These established violation types were in accordance with the letter and spirit of the OSHA Act until 1989, when the first unclassified was issued.[5] Since then, thousands of citations originally classified as willful, serious and repeat have been re-labeled as unclassified. OSHA's own database reveals an average of 552 unclassifieds per year, most issued by federal OSHA.[6]

Following a worker death, nothing terrifies senior management like the words "willful citation." Only when a citation is deemed willful does criminal prosecution become an option because the employer knowingly disregarded the law and exposed someone to a deadly hazard. While fear of criminal prosecution is perhaps the ultimate motivator behind negotiating citation types, so too is the fact that citation type bears directly on penalty amount, future litigation, and company image.

Unclassified citations are the result of backroom deals made between OSHA and employers caught violating worker health and safety regulations. In the case of Crouse-Hinds, the compliance officer wrote up 63 assorted willful violations, serious violations, and other-than-serious violations.[7] Then, OSHA and Crouse-Hinds' corporate attorneys made a deal to classify them under one long unclassified citation.

Crouse-Hinds is a division of Cooper Industries, a 4.5 billion dollar worldwide manufacturer of electrical parts, tools and hardware.[8] In the Syracuse, New York plant, a Crouse-Hinds employee was crushed to death when a mixing machine started while he was inside it. OSHA's electrical safety standard (lock-out/tag-out) specifically regulates this hazard of unexpected energy and equipment start-up. The actual case file shows that OSHA's compliance officer wrote up Crouse-Hinds for two willful violations of this well-known standard, each assigned the highest penalty amount of $70,000. Along with many others in the laundry list of citations, however, the two willfuls disappeared under the amorphous unclassified umbrella.

Many times, employers with catastrophic failures or chronic violations are willing and eager to negotiate for an unclassified. The invention of the unclassified, however, undermines the entire premise of OSHA law—the desire to hold employers accountable for their behavior. It lets some of the worst offenders off the hook for repeat and willful violations.

Crouse-Hinds was not fined $350,000 solely because an employee was crushed to death. Instead, OSHA conducted a comprehensive inspection of the plant and found serious, multiple problems, like the one described as: "The drums moved horizontally along a track, while at the same time rotating in a circular catwalk next to the rotating parts to perform oiling and maintenance work. The hazard consists of employees falling into vats and being pulled under the water by the rotating drums."[9]

Or the burn hazard described as, "Employees hand dip tools and bits into hot wax kettle to provide a protective cover on the tool edge. Wax is melted in the pot at temperatures approaching 300 degrees Fahrenheit. Employees fingers are as close as 1 inch to the molten wax."[10]

OSHA's compliance officers hardly nit-picked Crouse-Hinds. In fact, a combined violation of 81 individual instances of hoist ratings and inspection problems received just one $2,500 penalty. The inspectors also lumped 61 instances of machine guarding problems into one violation with a single

$7,000 penalty. Nine instances of ungrounded electrical equip-
ment received one $1,500 penalty, and 11 instances of unguard-
ed live electrical parts garnered just one $2,000 penalty. These
types of grouped violations occur even without any corporate
attorney pressure.

After the dust settled, only two violations were deemed willful by the compliance officers.[11] For both, they documented: 1)
The employer was aware the condition was hazardous; 2) The
employer was aware the condition violates an OSHA standard;
3) The employer is aware of the requirement of the standard;
and 4) The employers actions were deliberate, voluntary, or
intentional, and reflected a purposeful disregard of their responsibility. In fact, one willful citation noted that an employee's
hand was amputated four months into the OSHA inspection for
a similar violation cited in 1994. Even so, along with the public absolution offered by the unclassified designation, the two
willful penalties were reduced from $70,000 to $5,500 each.

Since the 1999 fatality, Crouse-Hinds received three more
OSHA inspections and seven more unclassified citations.
Without the unclassified loophole, those citations would likely
have been willfuls or repeats. In fact, one appears originally in
OSHA's database as a repeat with a $7,500 fine.[12] It was negoti-
ated into an unclassified and discounted $2,500.

Because OSHA cuts deals on citation types and penalties,
companies get away with chronic non-compliance. Some would
say they get away with murder.

***

Weasel Words
Liability dodging extends beyond re-classifying citations.
The Crouse-Hinds citations, for example, were referred to in
the settlement agreement as "alleged."[13] Clearly, fear of further
prosecution from beyond OSHA—lawsuits from victim's fami-

lies—is a concern of violators, but OSHA has no right to accommodate employer fear with words like unclassified and alleged. OSHA's acquiescence takes from families the option to pursue civil litigation; it removes the potential for criminal prosecution; and it undermines the primary goal of OSHA to hold employers responsible for their workplaces.

The Crouse-Hinds settlement agreement includes other butt-covering clauses, like the section which read, "Characterizations. The violations alleged in the citation items are unclassified (i.e. not alleged to be willful, repeated, serious, or other.)" And the grand-daddy of them all, which read:

> No Admission of Liability or Fault. This Settlement Agreement is entered into solely to resolve disputes arising from the Inspection and all other matters within the scope of Paragraph 1, and thereby to avoid litigation and expense to the parties. Neither the Company nor Company officers or employees admit to any violations of the Act. The Company does not waive any claim or defense to the citations, and does not waive any defense or argument in future proceedings, including, but not limited to, the right to assert that any future conditions identical or similar to those alleged do not violate the Act. The citations, the penalty, the termination of this litigations, this Agreement or its execution, the abatement of alleged violations, the payment of any penalty, the waiver of the right to contest, as well as any final order resulting from this Agreement, shall not constitute an admission or evidence, shall not be deemed or construed in any court, agency, forum, or proceeding, state or federal, as an admission or evidence of any violation of the Act, or of fault or liability, or as an admission or evidence that any alleged condition

existed, that any violation occurred, or that any alleged violation caused or contributed to, proximately or otherwise, any accident, injury, illness or death that may have occurred, and shall not be an admission or evidence, in whole or in part, in any such forum, except that OSHA may use and enforce the final orders resulting herefrom in proceedings and matters arising directly under the Act.

Those types of ridiculously long, carefully worded paragraphs are included to make sure that the victim's family does not gain evidence of company wrongdoing. Since workers compensation protects employers from lawsuits, employers are careful to protect that shield; hence, the fancy legal footwork. Put another way, even though a man died and the company agreed to pay $350,000, Crouse-Hinds admits no fault.

A Paper Tiger's Roar

OSHA's watered-down enforcement can be partially explained, but not excused by its limited resources. OSHA is not large or well funded. At current funding, it is equipped with only 2,145 federal and state OSHA inspectors for the nation's seven million workplaces. Federal OSHA would need 107 years just to inspect each establishment once while the state OSHA's would require 60 years.[14]

In 1990, Congress increased the maximum penalties for OSHA violations to $7,000 for serious violations and to $70,000 for willful and repeat violations.[15] Those intimidating figures, however, dissolve during settlement agreements and negotiations. Despite the $70,000 willful penalty allowed, for example, they actually average less than half that—only about $23,000. Unclassifieds, presumably willfuls in sheep's clothing, come in at a shocking $8,900. Even worse, employers pay $650 for the average serious violation and only $2,900 for repeat violations.[16] With penalties this low and the risk of inspection so remote, it makes economic sense for many employers to risk a potential OSHA penalty rather invest in prevention.

With its small staff and budget, the strength of OSHA is not in its day-to-day enforcement threat. Like the IRS needs tax return audits, OSHA needs a big threat because it can't be everywhere at once. The real influencing force behind OSHA is employer fear of being made into a national headline, receiving maximum penalties, and facing criminal prosecution.

Nevertheless, when it created the unclassified violation, OSHA traded its enforcement threat for the ease of closed cases, less litigation, and faster resolution. As a result, OSHA is no longer the force it was created to be. The word is out that OSHA folds when the stakes get high.

Issuing unclassifieds and tolerating weasel words benefits OSHA by limiting legal costs and closing cases quickly. It benefits employers by not making them look willfully or repetitively negligent. The deal works for everyone except the families of dead workers. It also shortchanges workers everywhere because the agency designed to protect them is near death from poisoning its own system.

***

In August of 2000, I contacted the federal OSHA press office and requested an interview with the Solicitor's office. Among other things, I wanted to ask the agency's head lawyer where OSHA gets the legal authority to create a new type of violation, the unclassified, simply by writing it up in a memo and in the FIRM. Numerous follow-up attempts via telephone, letter and E-mail were made. I informed the public affairs office that if I heard from no one, I would state in the book that I was refused an interview and would draw my own conclusions. I was still waiting a year later.

During my wait, I checked other OSHA references for background on the unclassifieds, but it seems the agency is not discussing it. In fact, it appears they are hiding it.

OSHA's "All About OSHA" publication, for example, was just released in 2000 and describes the usual OSHA violations but says nothing about the unclassified.[17] OSHA's handbook on employer rights and responsibilities—the booklet left by compliance officers following an inspection—also fails to mention the unclassified citation. It lists just the traditional violation types, even though it was revised in 1999, ten years after the first unclassified was issued.[18]

Today, OSHA refers to unclassified citations as Section 17(c) citations because that section of the OSHA Act says that "any employer who has received a citation for a violation...and such violation is specifically determined not to be of a serious nature, may be assessed a civil penalty of up to $7,000 for each such violation." OSHA's internal policy manual describes the unclassified this way: "If an employer, having been cited as willfully or repeatedly violating the Act, decides to correct all violations, but wishes to purge himself or herself of the adverse public perception attached to a willful or repeated penalty and is willing to make significant additional concessions, then a Section 17 designation may be applicable. Decisions to make a Section 17 designation shall be based on whether the employer is willing to make significant concessions."[19] The problem is that the Act says nothing about trading "significant concessions" for avoidance of negative social stigma. OSHA just took it upon itself to create this compromise and offer a loophole.

In OSHA's policy manual, examples given of significant concessions were entering into a corporate-wide settlement agreement, hiring a safety and health consultant or beginning a safety and health program. A review of 25 actual OSHA case files, however, revealed few significant concessions. In some, the so-called concessions were steps companies should already be taking under current OSHA law.

In the Crouse-Hinds case, for example, the company agreed to hire a safety and health consultant. Instead of incrementally managing their life and limb-threatening operations, over time, Crouse-Hinds accumulated such a problematic workplace that they had to hire outside help. Then, they were given credit by OSHA for agreeing to do what they should have been doing all along. That is no concession.

As Ron forewarned, OSHA is not even complying with its own questionable policies. The OSHA policy manual says that unclassified violations can "be considered if the employer has advanced substantial reasons why the original classification is questionable but is willing to pay the penalty as proposed."[20] So, while Section 17(c) of the OSHA Act specifically refers strictly to violations *found not to be serious*, OSHA's policy manual ignores this and instead offers a trade for full penalty payment.

Furthermore, OSHA discounts unclassifieds an average of 27%,[21] hardly payment of the proposed penalty. Payment of an OSHA penalty is not supposed to be optional. Other enforcement agencies don't work that way. Tax evaders penalized by the IRS don't get perks for paying the fines they deserve. They don't get coddled with offers of protection from the social stigma they brought upon themselves. The Drug Enforcement Agency does not grant concessions to drug dealers that agree to no longer sell illegal drugs. The Security Exchange Commission does not accommodate insider stock trades by allowing cheaters to continue trading. Instead, violators of these laws are called criminals, and they get a record to prove it.

Adding to its illegitimacy, OSHA is issuing unclassifieds as initial citations when Section 17(c) of the OSHA Act refers strictly to citations found not to be serious. When unclassifieds are issued in the first place, they cannot later be found to be not serious.[22] Because employers don't want willful or repeat violations showing up in OSHA's IMIS database as initial cita-

tions—before they are even issued, before the compliance officer can even finish his/her paperwork—industry lawyers call
OSHA lawyers and get the deal underway. In these cases, unless
actual OSHA case files are reviewed, there is no way to know
what the compliance officer originally cited. Injured and ill
workers or families of deceased workers have no say in the matter. Most are unaware of the negotiations and violation types
until it is too late. Or, they never learn what happened.

Finally, in direct conflict with the Act's Section 17(c),
OSHA's policy manual blatantly states that unclassifieds may be
issued to "employers having been cited as willfully or repeatedly violating the Act."[23] OSHA is issuing unclassifieds for serious,
repeat and willful violations instead of those found later not to
be serious.[24]

This crazy section of OSHA's policy manual on the unclassified violation is taken verbatim from an August 14, 1991 letter
of interpretation, explaining why OSHA is supposedly allowed
to issue unclassifieds:

"The legislative history of Section 17 of the OSH Act,
which, as you know, is concerned with penalties, indicates that
the Congress devised the citation classification system outlined
in Section 17 so that penalties might be proposed and assessed
at various levels which would correspond to the nature and
severity of the violations found. In fact, Section 17 is the only
section of the Act that deals with violation classification. The
classification system there assumes that a recalcitrant employer
will only be dissuaded from further violation by a significantly
higher penalty as compared to first time violators. The legislative reason for classifying violations, therefore, is to enable the
Agency to propose a penalty appropriate to the violation."[25]

This interpretation ignores the intended social cost and stigma associated with the Act's pre-determined scale of violations,
and dismisses entirely the option of criminal prosecution for
willful citations. Those factors, in addition to the penalties,

serve as motivation *to all employers* to avoid future injuries and illnesses. They are the power of OSHA and the unclassifieds have undermined them.

The interpretive letter on unclassifieds also says, "If an employer, having been cited as willfully or repeatedly violating the Act, decides to correct all violations but wishes to purge himself of the adverse public perception attached to a willful or repeated violation classification and is willing to pay all or almost all of the penalty and to make other significant concessions, then the fundamental public purpose of the Act has been accomplished."[26]

But the fundamental purpose of the Act is to hold employers accountable for the health and safety of their workers. The Act is intended to put the fear of OSHA in employers that might not otherwise do the right thing. To grant them absolution from the stigma of serious, willful and repeat violations simply because they are willing to pay for it is a sell-out.

Furthermore, because the unclassified removes the potential for criminal prosecution, it cheats the families of dead workers of the peace that comes from knowing justice was served. When a willful is negotiated away, families not only suffer the tragic loss of a loved one, they suffer the indignation of being dismissed in favor of reduced legal fees, "significant concessions," and closed cases.

Crouse-Hinds paid a $350,000 penalty. Was it enough? The brother-in-law of the worker crushed to death was quoted in the local Syracuse newspaper as saying Crouse-Hinds "got away cheap. It should have been in the millions, so much that it hurt them. This doesn't resolve the issue for us. Every day I watch my family suffer because of what happened over there. A fine of $350,000 doesn't mean anything to us. We hope it teaches them a lesson on how to do things the right way."[27]

***

Industry loves the unclassified violation. A report on settlement agreements published by the reputable Bureau of National Affairs' Occupational Health and Safety Reporter in 1997 described the unclassified citation as, "among the most useful aspects of the settlement from the employer's perspective."[28]

Attorney George Salem defended Wyman-Gordon Forgings, Inc., an aerospace parts supplier investigated by OSHA after a 1996 explosion. The article explained:

> Personal injury litigation is a concern for the employers, according to management attorneys. Eight employees were killed and two injured in the blast at the Wyman-Gordon facility. According to Salem, the families of the dead and injured have a plaintiffs' committee made up of seven or eight attorneys who are watching the OSHA case to see how it is resolved. The fact that citations are not classified, and that the settlement amount was 1.8 million when single fatality cases have been assessed multimillion-dollar penalties, will provide the plaintiffs with "more realistic expectations" about damages in their own individual cases, Salem said.[29]

In the article, Salem summed up the unclassified situation by recommending industry attorneys do all they can to make settlement possible to avoid the potential liability faced by employers when an employee is killed or injured. He described the unclassified settlement as a "package that is acceptable from the perspective of collateral litigation."

The 'good news' of OSHA's unclassified citation has spread. On its website, for example, a law firm advertised their success with major safety, health and environmental investigations with the following brag:

> Represented large shipyard in defending against OSHA wall-to-wall inspection and negotiating subsequent reduction of willful citations to unclassified with over 50% reduction of seven-figure penalty, including resolution of abatement issues

relating to over 400 items involving scaffold construction, guardrail usage, and injury and illness recordkeeping.

Negotiated pre-citation settlement (with a 90% reduction in the proposed OSHA fine and a resolution with the Justice Department and state district attorney of potential criminal willful issues) in connection with a proposed eight figure fine arising from a wall-to-wall inspection at a large meat processing facility that suffered a triple fatality.

Negotiated with OSHA settlement agreement for chemical company faced with fourteen proposed serious and two willful items—agreement reduced citations to six unclassified items and included unprecedented exculpatory language helpful to the defense of collateral tort litigation.

Handled interface with numerous regulatory agencies including OSHA, state and federal prosecutors, and state and federal environmental agencies, regarding release of highly toxic chemical at chemical company that resulted in a one-week evacuation of a small town. Negotiated pre-citation OSHA settlement agreements citing minimal violations unrelated to causation of the release.[30]

***

Disposable Human Beings

Garrett saw his co-worker get pulled into a mullerator, an eight to nine-foot long cylinder with a 6-inch steel shaft running through the center of it. The shaft had numerous arms with blades attached to mix the sand that ran through it. Every night it was cleaned and serviced because the blades had to be set at 3/16th of an inch from the outside walls to best mix the sand. The death Garrett witnessed was in a machine similar to that at Crouse-Hinds.

There were two mullerators, Garrett explained. One person was cleaning one and another person was servicing the other. The person cleaning the machine often "jogged it" to move the blades slightly to get to the different parts. He accidentally "jogged" the wrong machine, pulling the other worker into it.

"He was taken almost three-quarters of the way around. He had to have been killed instantly." Garrett said. "It was the worst thing I ever saw in my life."

The mullerators were cleaned and serviced every night and the employer knew it. Reaching into a blade-filled chamber is unarguably a recognized hazard, the very type the OSHA Act was designed to address. Still, OSHA fined them $455.

When Garrett heard this, he said, "Something as easy as separating the control panels or a lockout for this to not have happened is amazing. Then the OSHA report of only a $455.00 fine negotiated down from some other amount was totally outrageous. We are just numbers in a hat that can be replaced at the drop of a dime."

This same sentiment—feeling disposable—was echoed by two of Garrett's coworkers who were also injured on the job. They say, "OSHA's been in the plant before and done nothing" so they don't expect improvements anymore. OSHA's inspection history at this site reveals six inspections since the mullerator fatality. Although a total of 25 violations were cited including 14 serious violations, total penalties reached a paltry $5,570.

To make steel tubes for their employer, these workers have to manually attach heavy steel coils to a wheel that dates from the civil war. They don't just have to lift the coil, they have to lift it and then shove it with force to get it onto the "payoff wheel."

Garrett is a big guy. He used his brawn for a living and admits, "I was one of those "It can't happen to me guys. With all the stitches and bruises I've had over the years, if I filed accident reports each time I'd have a book. I liked the physical part.

I always felt better doing heavy work so I that's what I did."

Garrett had sixteen years in at this same steel tube company—five years in the same department—before he "pulled a Michael Jackson move" on a grease and coolant slimed platform. He didn't fall but as his foot slid, he felt something pop in his back and pain seared through his leg. After he took his break a short while later, he says, "I couldn't get up."

Garrett's job involved lots of reaching but instead of building proper stairs and platforms with handrails, Garrett's employer simply laid down wooden pallets for employees to stand on. While the pallets served the purpose of raising employees, they had no handrails and were not really washable. They also cost less. It was on one of these makeshift pallet platforms that Garrett slid.

"We had those wooden platforms for two years and we complained the whole time. We had to climb up and down on them when a real walkway would have cost just $500. That ruined my life."

It was because Garrett relied so heavily on his physical abilities all his life that he lost a big piece of his self-worth along with the job and paycheck. He can't ride his lawn mower, crawl under a leaking sink or even do heavy cleaning without his back beginning to hurt. He can't sit in a car for more than thirty minutes. He has lost 40 pounds since he stopped working. Being physically and financially unable to contribute to his family and home has left him feeling worthless. That, plus the pain and the legal problems (his lawyer just asked him for $1,000 for half the neurologist's deposition fee) have led to depression.

Wearing the "injured worker label" only adds to the burden. Garrett describes a safety meeting that began with the plant manager threatening, "If workers' comp keeps going the way its going, the plant will close in two years." Although Garrett's employer is self-insured, the employer still does not implement safer equipment or procedures. Instead, injured workers become the enemy, a risk and threat to their coworkers. Garrett said, "It pits the union workers against the injured workers. They look at me like I am a fake, like I can't really be hurt because I'm so big."

The steel tubes that make our hammocks, grills, bikes, chairs and cables do not reflect the costs, pain and suffering paid by Garrett or the risks borne by the more than three hundred workers still employed at this company at this same location.

Garrett says, "We have sent people to the moon for thirty years, and in our plant, we have guys standing on one leg pushing 1800-pounds of steel coil."

***

The Big Picture—A Collage of Compromise

OSHA Area Directors are the routine decision-makers for Informal Settlement Agreements. The regional solicitor's office weighs in when a case can't be settled informally, and when cases are formally contested, Administrative Law Judges in the OSHA Review Commission take over. They are all issuing unclassifieds, discounting penalties, and reclassifying citations.

State run OSHA's are not required to adopt all of federal OSHA's procedures; they must simply run as stringently as federal OSHA. Regarding unclassifieds, however, state run OSHA's are running more stringently.

The 24 state run OSHA's rarely issue unclassifieds. In Fiscal Year 1999, state run OSHAs issued 6 unclassifieds, although that number creeped to 46 in Fiscal Year 2000. An assistant director from a state run OSHA hypothesized that state plans don't need to issue unclassifieds because they have richer resources compared to federal OSHA. Admitting that willfuls are hard to prove, he noted that their state will sometimes negotiate a serious instead. "We negotiate settlements, but we don't issue unclassifieds."

Unclassifieds are only one piece of the employer/OSHA

negotiation. Area directors are authorized to change abatement dates, to reclassify violations, and to modify or withdraw a penalty, a citation or a citation item if they become convinced that the changes are justified."[31]

Some discretion is indeed necessary. In West Virginia, for example, a compliance officer found two employees working in a trench showing evidence of an impending cave-in. A protective trench box was lying on the ground right next to the trench, but the workers decided not to put it in the excavation.

The compliance officer wrote in his notes that he called the owner, a man who had been in the trenching business for 29 years and understood OSHA's trenching regulations. Describing their conversation, the compliance officer wrote, "He was awfully aggravated, that the employees are older guys that had been with the company for years, that he himself had performed an inspection of the jobsite just yesterday, and the very same operator on this job was in the trench box without a ladder and he gave him hell for not using the ladder. He stated that after all the training they provide these guys, they have three day sessions where everyone goes for training and they also do one day training, plus tool box talks. That they know that this is not the company policy."

The compliance officer did not cite the employer for lack of a written electrical safety program, something observed during the inspection, but did cite the employer for not complying with the trenching requirement to have a competent person inspect the jobsite. No penalty, however, was issued with the competent person citation. Although workers were clearly exposed to a potentially life-threatening hazard, the compliance officer wrote up only two citations with penalties. The first was a serious violation for $1,500 for not using a protective system in the trench. The second was also a serious violation for $1,500 for placing the excavated dirt within two feet of the trench edge, thereby increasing odds for a cave-in.

So, before any citations were issued, the compliance officer essentially dismissed the electrical program and competent person requirements. The inspector also reduced the two penalties that would be issued to acknowledge the employer's small size. OSHA routinely reduces penalty amounts based on employer size—60% for employers with 1 to 25 employees; 40% for employers with 26-100 employees; 20% for firms with 101-250 employees and zero discount for firms with more than 250 employees.[32]

On top of the small business discount, the employer then met with the local area director who agreed to an informal settlement. The first penalty for not using the trench box was changed to an unclassified, and the penalty was further reduced to $1,125. The second citation was deleted, as was its penalty. The employer sent a check for $1,125.

While this employer arguably deserved the small business discount and perhaps the waiver for a missing electrical safety program, he was not required to provide "significant concessions" or pay the full penalty in exchange for the unclassified violation. More importantly, the cited hazard was never deemed less than serious. Should this same company have a trench cave-in or future violation trenching violations, repeat or willful citations won't be issued.

Citation deletions are as important an issue as unclassifieds. Deletions are not errors or oversights; they are actual removals of both penalty and violation after the citation has been issued. Once a citation has been issued, OSHA can delete it entirely or essentially delete it by merging it into another citation. From 1989 to 1999, OSHA deleted an average of 13,626 violations per year.[33] This number excludes preliminary decisions made by compliance officers, as in the trenching case, to simply leave violations off the paperwork. This practice, in addition to the unclassifieds, leads to under-citing repeat and willful violations. The OSHA Act is not being enforced as the public believes it is.

In Waupaca, WI, a man fell 50 feet to his death when he stepped between steel beams to avoid a falling piece of 15 foot by 15 foot piece of foundry wall. He wore no fall protection, and the beams were wet and covered with dust.

The compliance officer wrote up 2 serious citations and 4 willfuls with an assigned penalty of $79,000. After the settlement agreement, the employer received an unclassified with a 29% penalty reduction.[34]

The notes from the informal conference reveal the employer's position: "Willful—perception, looks like intentional effort caused death, and causes problems with future bidding problems...discussed section 17 designation of violation.... Willfulness affects ability to get jobs—company has made a lot of effort and citation demeans these efforts..."

These employer concerns are valid. They made a mistake and are facing very real consequences but at least those sitting in the meeting were not killed. They are not suffering the sudden and needless loss of a family member. Instead, they face only financial loss.

The employer's concerns, however legitimate, are essentially irrelevant. Local OSHA agencies exist to enforce the OSHA Act, not to sympathize with or rationalize away the consequences employers bring upon themselves. Even the threat of litigation should not sway support from a compliance officer's documented findings.

The same meeting notes show why the local OSHA area director compromised. Taken almost verbatim from the interpretation letter on unclassifieds, the area director wrote, "Changing willful to Section 17 avoids litigation over name of the citation— significance of the violation reflected in the penalty."

Further, next to a note in the margin titled "basis to reduce penalty," the area director wrote: "Company contention that foreman coming from union hall being employee misconduct—

company can show disciplinary action on other jobs, not likely to get a penalty this high if case litigated." This employer was fortunate that the foreman on duty that day had a disciplinary record. No mention was made, however, as to whether that record or the foreman's behavior contributed to the worker's death. Also not mentioned was how either of those factors absolved the employer from their ultimate responsibility for a safe worksite.

On that same worksite, the compliance officer found employees working off an extension ladder placed upon a wooden sheet which was clamped to structural steel in only one place. Regarding the willful citation written by the compliance officer, the area director wrote: "Company believed ladder was stable and saw no problem working off the ladder. Since this is a judgment issue, would be difficult to prove willful in court." OSHA has reached a new low when the agency fears their judgment will be overridden by that of a construction company with an haphazard scaffold and a recent fatality. Instead, the more likely reason is the cost and bother of fighting for the willful. "Difficult to prove willful in court" translates into "let it go."

Although an unclassified was issued, no "significant concessions" were noted in either the discussion from the informal conference or in the informal settlement agreement. In fact, the informal conference notes state that the employer had already "extended supervisor training, knowledge in management responsibilities" but then that same requirement appeared in the informal settlement agreement to supposedly require the employer "to conduct an orientation for new foreman which delineates their responsibilities as representatives of management." It is already an OSHA requirement that employers placing workers in charge of potentially life-threatening operations train them adequately.

***

> OSHA proposes over $66,000 in penalties against
> Clean Harbors Environmental Services, Inc., for alleged
> willful and serious violations following explosion at
> Norwalk, Conn., worksite....OSHA's inspection found
> that this employer had failed to implement several basic
> safeguards for employees who were working on this site
> and whose duties involved entering the tanks....First of
> all, Clean Harbors did not implement a site-specific
> safety and health plan prior to starting this project. The
> plan would have identified the various hazardous sub-
> stances, such as methanol, toluene, methylene chloride,
> and various solvents and oils, on the jobsite and also
> evaluated and addressed the hazards posed to employees
> by those substances.
>
> —OSHA Region 1 Press Release,
> December 2, 1999

Only ten days after that press release was issued, OSHA
signed a settlement agreement, which revealed no significant
concessions and included a penalty reduction of $15,700.

Congress knows of the goings-on at OSHA. Just one 1996
report informs Congress of both OSHA's unclassified violations
and the fact that final penalty amounts are essentially useless.
Submitted by the GAO, the report analyses occupational safety
and health violations by federal contractors. In order to study the
significance of OSHA's violations, the GAO relied only on the
Compliance Officer's proposed penalty "because they are based
on the compliance officer's judgment of the nature and severity of
violations, while actual penalties may be the product of other factors such as negotiations between OSHA and the company to
encourage quicker abatement of workplace hazards."[35]

Later in the report, Congress is told: "OSHA characterizes
violations as other-than-serious, serious, willful, or repeat, with
civil penalties in specified increasing amounts for these various
types of violations. In addition, OSHA designates violations as

unclassified when companies make significant concessions to OSHA, perhaps to avoid losing coverage under state workers' compensation programs or to minimize adverse publicity attached to violations as originally classified."[36] Apparently, these statements caused little distress in the halls of Congress because nothing has changed.

CHAPTER 9

The Cure = Information + Exposure

The Freedom of Information Act (FOIA)

"I call it the Fighting for Information Act. There's nothing free about it. The time and money expended to get a few documents is unbelievable."[1] says Ron Hayes. He should know. For each grieving family Hayes helps, he submits a FOIA request to OSHA so the family can read the records on their loved ones.

"It is healing to understand exactly what happened. Families have so many questions, they are confused as well as grief-stricken. Reading the OSHA files helps them understand exactly what happened and why, and they get some peace from it. But OSHA won't release the files until the case is closed, and by then the penalties and citations are settled. That's intentional."

Since Independence Day of 1966 when FOIA was passed, reporters and citizens alike have had better access to all sorts of government information. Under OSHA, FOIA is the main tool for affected families and the media to gain information. The problem is that OSHA's FOIA process is broken. This leaves the public in the dark.

With no cooperation or response from federal OSHA's Office of the Solicitor, I decided to let the facts speak for themselves. To gain insight on the actual behavior of OSHA, I submitted a FOIA request for 25 complete, actual case files from federal OSHA offices all over the country.[2] The cases were selected from a list of companies that had received unclassifieds.

The FOIA law requires government agencies to respond to requests within twenty days, letting the requestor know whether the request will be complied with. OSHA generally responds within twenty days by sending a form letter acknowledging receipt of the request but can, and usually does, take months to actually process the request. The form letter does not indicate a determination of whether or what information will be released. This is OSHA's first major side-step of the FOIA Act. Sending a form letter within twenty days is not the same as responding to the request within twenty days.

Months passed before any of the requested files trickled in. When they did arrive, they were incredibly inconsistent. Several offices sent the bare minimum file, stuffed with a few generic forms to bulk it up. Some tried to pass off a few forms as a complete file.[3] A few appeared to be almost complete files, including copies of hand-written meeting notes, case logs and even copies of local newspaper articles. On average, though, the predominant response was to provide the smallest, safest amount of information with a cover letter telling me I could file an appeal if I did not like what I got.

According to OSHA, "OSHA policy is to disclose all documents to which the public is entitled under the Freedom of Information Act and the regulations, including those where an exemption may apply if it is in the public interest to do so and does not impede the discharge of any of the functions of the agency, unless disclosure of such documents is prohibited."[4] Under FOIA, there are allowable exemptions, such as when information may compromise privacy, impede justice, or interfere with government function. Much information, however, is supposed to be made public. Since all the requested cases were closed, the only real exemption should have been to protect privacy, which would have allowed deletions such as employee names, phone numbers and other individual identifiers.

Instead, in almost all of the twenty-five files, OSHA went crazy with omissions and deletions. For example, form OSHA-1 is the inspection report, and according to OSHA's own internal FOIA procedure, "all items on OSHA-1 form are disclosable.[5] Some case files received, however, included sections of OSHA-1 blacked out.[6] In addition, most files excluded entire documents that should have been released, including: employee interviews, fatality/catastrophe reports, correspondence, and witnesses' statements.

OSHA's inconsistent and often reluctant release of information conflicts directly with the intent of FOIA and OSHA's own policies. Without timely, open access to OSHA happenings, the media can't effectively inform the public. The media can not adequately report on local businesses or injuries and illnesses if OSHA takes six months or longer to release information—information that may be incomplete. By then, the story is too old.

Without the media and reliable reporting, the public won't be informed or outraged at what OSHA, Congress, and businesses are up to. In large part, this lack of public oversight has contributed to the deplorable condition of our nation's workplace health and safety. Turned around, it can also lead to the cure.

If the public were more informed of the vital need for OSHA, more support might be provided to the struggling agency. Also, public scrutiny of OSHA and industry activity can not only rectify undesirable behavior like the current unclassified trend, it can prevent such activities in the first place. If industry knew their OSHA files might be discussed in a book or news article, perhaps they would run safer and healthier workplaces to begin with. Investors, consumers and employees could choose to go elsewhere when they learn of a company's poor safety and health practices. Likewise, employers known for their commitment to keep their employees safe and healthy could attract greater business.

Thorough, fast FOIA responses are critical to informing the public about both OSHA and corporate behavior. FOIA is already an existing law and simply complying with it is one of the cheapest, effective and immediate solutions the public and Congress could demand.

***

Fighting for Information

Under FOIA, the public has a legal right to know what is going on. This right is especially important with agencies like OSHA that govern health and welfare. These agencies should not only be willing to open its file drawers, if they are doing a good job then they should welcome and encourage in-depth exposure. With OSHA, the agency limits information until cases are closed and then generally releases files only by formal FOIA request. Many of those will require lengthy appeals in order to get all the disclosable information. It is hardly an open process.

As the author of a book intended to benefit the public with essentially no commercial interest, I was eligible for a fee waiver for copying and processing charges.[7] A fee waiver request was included in my original FOIA letter to OSHA's Washington, DC headquarters. It was then forwarded with my letter from Washington to all offices responsible for responding with local case files. Several of the OSHA area offices requested further, written justification for the fee waiver, but all ultimately granted it—with the exception of one.

My request for the Jahn Foundry Corp. file was received in the Springfield, MA Area Office on November 24, 2000. One month later, the Area Director, sent a letter stating "We are in the process of locating and processing the requested records and will forward them to you as soon as possible. I anticipate that there will be a delay of approximately four to six weeks." Four months passed. Then, the Area Director sent a letter notifying me that the FOIA processing fee would be $1,726.70, required in advance, to cover "....the professional and administrative time as well as the cost of reproducing the 7,653 available pages of information."

I sent in the same written justification that had been accepted by the other offices, informing the Area Director that all the other offices had accepted my fee waiver status. He was not swayed. I offered to discuss the file contents to exclude unnecessary items and reduce processing time. (No other file exceeded 400 pages, most were less than 100.) After several letters and phone calls, on May 1, 2000—six months after my original request to Washington—the Area Director refused to grant my FOIA fee waiver on the basis that "this request is for information that meets the definition of a commercial use request, as it is clearly intended to further your commercial interests."

Despite the fact that I received no advance from my publisher and had virtually no chance of recovering the lost salary and personal savings invested in this book, I was refused the Jahn Foundry file without a $1,762.70 check. The primary OSHA FOIA officer in Washington agreed it would be "out of the question" for me to be forced into submitting tax returns and expense reports in order to prove my nonexistent "commercial interest." (Indeed, if I truly had a commercial interest and expected to make money off this book, I would have just sent a check.) Still, she said, Area Directors are allowed to determine FOIA requests on a case-by-case basis.

Unclassifieds had been issued initially to Jahn Foundry Corp. after an explosion killed three people and hospitalized nine. Of the mere $115,000 penalty issued to Jahn Foundry Corp., one unclassified had a penalty of $70,000, indicating it had likely been a willful. I can not report what, if any, "significant concessions" were traded by Jahn Foundry for their unclassified citation because I could not pay the fee, and the OSHA office refused to release the file without payment.

Granted, Jahn Foundry Corp. was one out of 25 files, but this treatment should not happen at all, let alone six months after a formal FOIA request. Stalling for six months and then demanding a huge processing fee is inexcusable. The Jahn Foundry case demonstrates how OSHA can impede the public's right to information, how it can undermine the intent of the FOIA law, and how it can disregard its own written policies.

In addition to the Jahn Foundry Corp. experience, two files took 6 months to produce. Although a Pennsylvania office logged in my request, they had no idea why I never received the file and, after a few phone calls, they eventually produced it. A Colorado office said it simply took that long to process because, "We had lots of fatalities and accidents last year and have had many FOIA requests as a result."

Whether the cause is human error, poor training, inadequate time, or intentional with-holding of information, OSHA's current FOIA practices are unacceptable. This is no way to treat a function so important to the public and to the families of injured, ill or killed workers.

Understaffed and poorly trained FOIA personnel are a real problem in OSHA. Several FOIA personnel expressed frustration with the lack of time they had to process files—each file has to be individually reviewed for exemptions like trade secrets or medical information—and then photocopied. A federal FOIA officer, and more than one local officer, stressed how little FOIA training they get and how FOIA responsibilities are usually added to a person's existing job with little or no more time made available. Many expressed faith in the agency but stressed that a lack of training was responsible for many of their internal processing problems.

In some instances, I suspect information was intentionally withheld because it was damning to the agency. In fact, one frustrated information officer in an OSHA area office flatly warned me that the FOIA information I would receive would be partially blacked out because "the government will remove what will embarrass us." He also admitted that the compliance officers need more training on health and safety and also on the legal aspects. "They are not trained too well," he said. "And they have to do so many inspections but the more you do, the more spread out you are and the less thorough each investigation is. There is pressure to remove the willful violations because they are hard to prove and the OSHA lawyers won't even take a case unless it is airtight. Besides, if a case is contested, we just lose it to the Administrative Law Judge. OSHA is spread so thin and companies hold them on every technicality. But the unclassified violations, those are definitely issued so the public doesn't see a willful," he said.

Another local FOIA officer adamantly stressed that OSHA's intentions are first to protect worker health and safety. In order to abate hazards quickly, she explained, OSHA will negotiate. Still, although speedy abatement is indeed a valid concern, it does not justify the extreme goings-on in OSHA like the issuance of unclassifieds, low penalties and questionable FOIA practices.

Since state OSHA's generally do not issue unclassifieds, I wondered if they suffered higher contested case rates. They do not. In fiscal year 2000, employers receiving citations contested only 9.6% of federal OSHA cases. During the same fiscal year, employers receiving citations from state run OSHA's only contested 4.7% more cases.[8] If federal OSHA eliminates unclassifieds, therefore, the rate of contested cases should—theoretically—not grow by more than 5%.

If OSHA eliminates its use of unclassifieds citations and complies consistently with its own procedures, odds are better that the agency would be more willing to reveal its case files and behind-the-scenes negotiations. If it were not afraid of exposure, the agency might comply more speedily and thoroughly to FOIA requests. To make a more open OSHA a reality, however, federal compliance officers must first be better trained on the legal and technical issues so that their cases can withstand contest. In addition, federal OSHA on the whole must be better supported by Administrative Law Judges, Congress, businesses and the public.

OSHA's Data Collection Initiative

It is not currently possible to learn which companies in the nation are the ones with the worst injury and illness rates. Although both the BLS and OSHA are part of the same department—the Department of Labor—the BLS staunchly refuses to release any employer specific information, including employer names, to OSHA or the public because it may inhibit employers from accurately providing data on injuries and illnesses. This is a valid, albeit frustrating and expensive, concern. As a result, the BLS only releases data categorized by type of industry, never revealing specific company names.

In recent years, OSHA began performing its own annual survey of about 80,000 businesses called the Data Collection Initiative (DCI.) This survey is used to determine who has the most dangerous workplaces so OSHA can target its inspections. The DCI, however, applies only to those employers already completing the OSHA recordkeeping forms which means that the same 5.5 million employers exempt from the BLS data collection are also exempt from the DCI. So, while two separate agencies within the same government department redundantly survey employers for workplace safety and health information, neither get the big picture. Still, OSHA's DCI is the only national injury and illness data other than the imperfect BLS data.

OSHA's DCI data includes the average annual number of employees and the total number of hours that employees worked during the previous calendar year. It also includes injury and illness information that employers have readily available on their OSHA logs. This information allows OSHA to calculate what is called a lost workday injury and illness rate (LWDII) for each particular establishment in the survey. Since the number of work hours is factored into the equation, the rates are comparable between employers. OSHA then targets employers with high rates for inspection.

The national average rate for lost workday injuries and illnesses is three per 100 full time employees. OSHA's targeted inspection program focuses on employers with eight or more injuries and illnesses per 100 employees.[9] Out of the 13,000 employers with LWDII rates exceeding eight, OSHA schedules inspections at the very worst, employers with rates of 13 or higher.[10]

Using the DCI data, OSHA can focus on workplaces where it can do the most good, while minimizing attention on employers already protecting their employees. The DCI is a good idea. It would be better if OSHA would release the DCI data to the public. It won't.

***

Matthew Carmel's business is numbers. Ten years ago, he started OSHA DATA, a private company where he could combine his penchant for computers, entrepreneurial spirit, and technical expertise, which includes a master's degree in environmental health engineering and board certifications in both industrial hygiene and safety. Not affiliated with any government agency, including federal OSHA, OSHA DATA offers clients the unique service of finding or calculating OSHA information.

Unless you know where to look, certain safety information can be hard to find—things like how often a company has been cited, why and for how much. To obtain or calculate such information, Matt submits quarterly, written requests to OSHA for a copy of IMIS, its master computer database. Under FOIA, OSHA has had to provide him with most of the requested information.

The companies that hire Matt value his service. They either don't know where to look, haven't got the time to look, or don't know how to calculate or interpret the data that Matt offers.

Attorneys representing injured workers hire Matt and ask "Did OSHA ever cite his employer for this before?" Reporters call Matt when they write about local fires or fatalities; Matt can quickly tell them the company's OSHA history and interpret it. The City of New York hires Matt to provide information on its subcontractors before hiring them to ensure public safety. They have done this ever since the tragic death of a child hit by a falling brick while walking under one of the City's construction projects. Although OSHA Data is not a non-profit organization, it provides a public service by providing fast, understandable information about health and safety performance.

Twice, Matt was willing to go to court to get OSHA's DCI data and twice OSHA was willing to go to court to refuse to give it to him. Now, when Matt calls OSHA for technical information, some researchers are so concerned about even speaking with him that they don't return his phone calls. He once left a technical question for a researcher at the OSHA laboratory in Salt Lake City, and OSHA's legal department called back wanting to know what he wanted. A member of the Washington DC press office once literally cursed and screamed at him on the phone. If there is an OSHA blacklist, Matt is near the top. This is a sad statement about OSHA. Not only is the agency less than forthright, it appears fearful and hostile.

I went to Matt because I wanted to define the workplace epidemic with real situations and examples. I asked him questions like: "Which were the dangerous companies? Which are the safer and healthier companies? What type of work do they do? Were bigger companies safer? Are there trends in different states?"

Matt can't answer any of these questions because these are the two lawsuits he lost. Although OSHA's DCI surveys 80,000 companies each year on their safety performance, they will not release the data. They refused to release the DCI data to Matt as a commercial entity. Then they refused to release it to me as a member of the press writing for the public interest.

OSHA is a government entity paid by taxpayers to protect taxpayers. We have a right to know if employers are held accountable for workplace health and safety, and if OSHA is doing a good job. We also have an inherent right to know if the company we are applying to for a job has a record of killing or sickening people. Without the DCI data, there is no feasible way to check up on dangerous businesses or on OSHA.

It is for exactly the same reason that I asked for OSHA's DCI data—to shine the spotlight on the most dangerous companies—that OSHA won't release it. If they did, it would be political suicide.

I pleaded with a senior member in OSHA's statistics office, "But public pressure could improve safety and health. If people knew, they might not buy a company's product, use their services or buy their stock. They could choose not to work there. Bad publicity is an incentive to make the workplace safer."

The response: "You don't have to preach to me. It's the current climate in Congress. Certain large employers would immediately sue us and we will lose our support, our funding. Companies have already told us how tough it would be to hire people if the DCI data gets out. We've taken a stance not to release the DCI data. You'll have to submit FOIA requests."

I offered options. What if you give me the data for just the top offenders? What if you tell me only the rates of the companies? What if you don't tell me the number of workers but instead provide them by size ranges? What if you only release previous data from earlier years? By the end of the six-month exchange, I had submitted four FOIA requests and received three denials and one refusal.[11]

It makes sense for OSHA information—things like compliance reports, fines and inspection data—to be available to the public. To be fair, some of it is. FOIA requests for individual files can be submitted if you have the time to wait for a response and the money to pay for processing. More convenient is the federal OSHA website, which offers scads of free information, including regulations, guidelines, interpretation, letters, and recommendations. And, for those that know about it, part of OSHA's IMIS database is available online, and it does provide inspection information if users search by specific company name. IMIS does not, however, provide lost workday injury and illness rates; therefore, employers can not be compared. It is also not an easy tool to work with. (See endnote [12] for instructions and an example of how to start using online IMIS.)

The DCI data, however, is easier. It could be made available on the internet so people everywhere can look up one simple number to get an idea of how well a company protects its employees. Graduating students looking for work could use the DCI data to evaluate risks at different companies. Consumers could choose to patronize businesses with low injury and illness rates, and annual reports could include a company's LWDII rate compared with its competition. Releasing the DCI data would provide incentive to those businesses needing improvement while, at the same time, rewarding those companies steadfastly managing workplace safety and health.

Releasing the DCI data would cost taxpayers nothing and improve the health and welfare of workers all over the country. Taxpayers already pay to collect the same information *twice*, once by the BLS and again by OSHA. They ought to get to see it.

***

OSHA is de-motivated, under-funded, under-staffed, and—in many cases—poorly trained. The agency is paralyzed by fear of expensive, drawn-out industry lawsuits and increasing criticism from Congress. One result of OSHA's constant struggle—the undermined enforcement brought about by unclassified citations and compromising settlement agreements—has, in large part, ruined the agency. Adding to OSHA's speed of descent is the broken FOIA process and lack of public awareness and support.

Congress shares much, if not all, of the responsibility for OSHA's state. The fact that many of the state-run OSHA's fare better than federal OSHA speaks volumes about Congress' performance as Manager and CEO of OSHA. Time and time again, Congress takes steps to thwart OSHA rather than help it, such as when it sensationalized the home office inspection issue; stuck prohibitive riders on the agency's budget; ignores illness surveillance problems; and overturned the ergonomics standard. OSHA's not kidding when it says it fears retaliation were it ever to release the DCI data; much of it would come from Congress.

The problem is complicated and so the solution will be. It is not, for example, solely OSHA's fault and cannot be quickly fixed with an infusion of funds (although that would help if provided along with greater public oversight). Employers, on the other hand, could dramatically improve the situation by intentionally and aggressively managing occupational health and safety. Even if employers just decided to comply with the regulations currently on the books, that would be an enormous step forward from where we are now. Most importantly, industry leaders need to stop fighting improvements in Washington and spinning the issues to mislead the public and the workforce.

***

Only when the nation recognizes the true depth and impact of the workplace epidemic, as a country and as individuals, can we begin to take responsibility to control risk and reduce occupational deaths, injuries and illnesses. As an informed public, we can encourage greater corporate responsibility. As a motivated public, we can command a place at the table and bring the occupational health discussion out of the exclusive realm of the political and scientific community. As employers and employees, voters and leaders, we can choose to act responsibly, intelligently, and morally to protect human life and well-being.

Following the comprehensive, factual, and digested information on the environment made available in Rachel Carson's 1962 Silent Spring, America became aware of and is to this day interested in environmental issues. Like the environment, workplace health and safety carries both personal and community health, economic and political impact. Like the environment, occupational health and safety impacts all Americans and yet is often out of the control of those most at risk. Like the environment, millions of dollars are at stake as well as a priceless commodity—human health and safety.

Citizens concerned for the environment instituted both immediate and long term change in pollution prevention. To this day, the public generally manages to keep businesses on their environmental toes. Public interest groups maintain the momentum to keep the environment a public issue of national concern. It is time for the nation to likewise recognize and push occupational health to the forefront. There simply is no other force to stop it. Left alone, the epidemic raging through our nation's workplaces will continue as it has for decades. Or it will worsen.

Endnotes

Chapter 1

1 Leigh, J. Paul et al. Costs of Occupational Injuries and Illnesses. Ann Arbor: University of Michigan Press, 2000. pg. 1-2.

2 Leigh, J. Paul et al. Costs of Occupational Injuries and Illnesses. Ann Arbor: University of Michigan Press, 2000. pg. 13.

3 Leigh, J. Paul et al. Costs of Occupational Injuries and Illnesses. Ann Arbor: University of Michigan Press, 2000. pg. 1-2.

4 Leigh, J. Paul et al. Costs of Occupational Injuries and Illnesses. Ann Arbor: University of Michigan Press, 2000. footnote 1 for Chapter 1, page 259.

5 Leigh, J. Paul et al. Costs of Occupational Injuries and Illnesses. Ann Arbor: University of Michigan Press, 2000. pg. 1.

6 Leigh, J. Paul et al. "Occupational Injury and Illness in the United States: Estimates of Costs, Morbidity, and Mortality." Archives of Internal Medicine157; July 28, 1997: 1557-1568. A difficult number to prove, the 165 occupational illness deaths often result from exposures that occurred years earlier. Occupational illnesses often misdiagnosed and underreported.

7 Bureau of Labor Statistics, Census of Fatal Occupational Injuries. "Perils in the Workplace." Compensation and Working Conditions, Vol. 2, No. 3 Fall. 1997.

8 National Safety Council. Safety Culture and Effective Safety Management. Edited by George Swartz, Chapter by Eric Van Fleet. Chicago, IL. National Safety Council Press. pg. 125-126.

9 National Safety Council. Safety Culture and Effective Safety Management. Edited by George Swartz, Chapter by James Howe. Chicago, IL. National Safety Council Press. pg. 262.

10 Department of Labor, OSHA. e-Compliance Assistance Tools, Safety and Health Management. Module 1, Safety and Health Statistics.

11 Department of Labor, OSHA. "Success Stories, OSHA Saves Lives." http://www.osha.gov/oshinfo/success.html

12 In 1994, the latest statistic available. Department of Labor, OSHA. The Benefits of Participating in VPP. http://www.osha.gov/oshprogs/vpp/benefits.html

13 Department of Labor, OSHA. e-Compliance Assistance Tools, Safety and Health Management. Module 1, Reducing the Costs of Accidents. http://www.osha-slc.gov/SLTC/safetyhealth_ecat/mod1_reducecosts.htm

14 Department of Labor, OSHA. e-Compliance Assistance Tools, Safety and Health Management. Cost Calculation Worksheet. Module 1. http://www.osha-slc.gov/SLTC/safetyhealth_ecat/mod1_estimating_costs.htm

15 Department of Labor, OSHA. 1996. $afety Pays factsheet. http://www.osha-slc.gov/SLTC/safetyhealth_ecat/images/safpay1.gif. Employers wishing to calculate their own profit costs can download a free software package from the OSHA website ($afety Pays) and punch in company specific numbers. Go to this page on the OSHA website—http://www.osha-slc.gov/dts/osta/oshasoft/safetwb.html

16 Levitt, Raymond E. and Nancy M. Samelson. Construction Safety Management. 2nd Ed. New York: John Wiley & Sons, Inc., 1993. pg. 1.

17 Department of Labor, OSHA. e-Compliance Assistance Tools, Safety and Health Management. Module 1, Safety and Health Statistics.

18 Leigh, J. Paul et al. Costs of Occupational Injuries and Illnesses. Ann Arbor:

University of Michigan Press, 2000. pg. 1.

Chapter 2

1 Rohrlich, Ted and Evelyn Larrubia, "Anti-Fraud Drive Proves Costly for Employees." Los Angeles Times. Aug. 7, 2000.
http://www.latimes.com/news/state/20000807/t000073833.html

2 Leigh, J. Paul et al. Costs of Occupational Injuries and Illnesses. Ann Arbor: University of Michigan Press, 2000. pg. 195-197.

3 National Broadcasting company, Inc. Dateline, NBC, May 29, 2000. Burrelle's Information Services, Burrell's Transcripts, No. 1124. pg. 1.

4 National Academy of Social Insurance. "Workers' Compensation: Benefits, Coverage, and Costs, 1997 - 1998 New Estimates." May, 2000.
http://www.nasi.org/WorkComp/1997-98Data/wc97-98rpt.htm. page 1.

5 National Broadcasting company, Inc. Dateline, NBC, May 29, 2000. Burrelle's Information Services, Burrell's Transcripts, No. 1124. pg. 3.

6 While the AFL-CIO is actually a federation of many different unions, it is referred to as a union to simplify the reference.

7 AFL-CIO. "Fraud, Fraud and More Fraud." Workers' Compensation Notes; Issue 2, 1998.

8 Leigh, J. Paul et al. Costs of Occupational Injuries and Illnesses. Ann Arbor: University of Michigan Press, 2000. pg 195.

9 Workers' Compensation Notes, AFL-CIO Department of Occupational Safety and Health, Issue 3-00, May/June 2000. pg. 1.

10 Stern, Robert. Personal communication, reprint permission given.

11 Harris, Marlys. "Workers Comp: Falling Down on the Job." Consumer Reports. February, 2000. pg. 29. (Since workers' compensation is not taxed, theoretically, workers don't need their full wages; hence the Commissions two-thirds pay recommendation.)

12 Supreme Court of the State of Florida. Case Number 90,703: Report of the Fourteenth Statewide Grand Jury. Report of Workers' Compensation Fraud, Findings Section (IV)(A)(1). July Term, 1997.

13 Supreme Court of the State of Florida. Case Number 90,703: Report of the Fourteenth Statewide Grand Jury. Report of Workers' Compensation Fraud, Findings Section (IV)(A)(4). July Term, 1997.

14 State of Wisconsin, Department of Workforce Development. "workers' Compensation Fraud is Low." Press Release, November 26, 1977.

15 State of Wisconsin, Department of Workforce Development. "Allegations of workers' Compensation Fraud." November 1, 2000.

16 Rohrlich, Ted and Evelyn Larrubia, "Anti-Fraud Drive Proves Costly for Employees." Los Angeles Times. Aug. 7, 2000.
http://www.latimes.com/news/state/20000807/t000073833.html

17 Leigh, J. Paul et al. Costs of Occupational Injuries and Illnesses. Ann Arbor: University of Michigan Press, 2000. pg. 12-13.

18 Leigh, J. Paul et al. Costs of Occupational Injuries and Illnesses. Ann Arbor: University of Michigan Press, 2000. pg 2 and 11.

19 Harris, Marlys. "Workers Comp: Falling Down on the Job." Consumer Reports. February, 2000. pg. 32.

20 Rand News Release. "Compensation for Worker Injuries Found Similar at Large and Small Firms Outcomes Are Inadequate and Inequitable in Both Cases, Rand Analysts

Say." Santa Monica, CA. August 30, 2000.

21　AFL-CIO, Death on the Job: The Toll of Neglect. Temporary Total Disability Benefits, 2001 and Workers' Compensation Comparisons, 2001.

22　AFL-CIO, Death on the Job: The Toll of Neglect. Workers' Compensation Comparisons, 2001.

23　Harris, Marlys. "Workers Comp: Falling Down on the Job." Consumer Reports. February, 2000. pg. 33.

24　Harris, Marlys. "Workers Comp: Falling Down on the Job." Consumer Reports. February, 2000. pg. 29.

25　Harris, Marlys. Phone interview, July 7, 2000.

26　Schrempf, D. W. (Bill). President and CEO of National Council on Compensation Insurance, Inc. Letter to the Editor of Consumer Reports. January 26, 2000. http://www5.ncci.com/nccisearch/News/CEOCorr/ceo125.htm

27　Tarpinian, Greg. Labor Research Council, Workers' Compensation Fraud: The Real Story, June, 1998. http://www.lra-ny.com/workers_comp/workerscompfraud.html#anchor15454763

28　correspondence—anonymous worker

29　NIOSH. "Performance Highlights of the national Institute for Occupational Safety and Health, 1995-1999." March 31, 2000. page 23.

30　National Institute of Medicine. "Safe Work in the 21st Century: Education and Training Needs for the Next Decade's Occupational Safety and Health Personnel." Washington, DC: National Academy Press, 2000. pg. 24.

31　interview correspondence—anonymous worker

32　National Academy of Social Insurance. "Workers' Compensation: Benefits, Coverage, and Costs, 1997-1998 New Estimates." May, 2000. http://www.nasi.org/WorkComp/1997-98Data/wc97-98rpt.htm.

33　Young, Julius. "Workers' Compensation Reform: Why Is It Needed?" Boxer & Gerson, 171-12th Street, Suite 100, Oakland, CA 94612. (510) 835-8870. (Article text taken from a white paper prepared by Doug Kim for the California Applicant's Attorney Association. Mr. Duncan testified before the SB 996 Conference Committee hearing on Temporary and Permanent Disability Benefits, on May 8, 2000 at the State Capitol, Sacramento, CA.) http:www.boxerlaw.com/bg04024b.htm.

34　reprinted with permission from Melissa Smith-Horn.

35　Tarpinian, Greg. Labor Research Council, Workers' Compensation Fraud: The Real Story, June, 1998. http://www.lra-ny.com/workers_comp/workerscompfraud.html#anchor15454763

Chapter 3

1　Skrzycki, Cindy. "At EPA, Pollution Control Becomes a Family Concern." Washington Post. 15 Mar. 1994, pg. D01

2　Federal Register #: 65:23059-23081, April 24, 2000. Semi Annual Regulatory Agenda, OSHA Unified Agenda. Long Term Actions 2162. Indoor Air Quality in the Workplace, http://www.osha-slc.gov/Reg_Agenda_data/2162.html

3　Federal Register #: 65:23059-23081, April 24, 2000. Semi Annual Regulatory Agenda, OSHA Unified Agenda. Long Term Actions 2162. Indoor Air Quality in the Workplace, http://www.osha-slc.gov/Reg_Agenda_data/2162.html

4　NIOSH Pocket Guide to Chemical Hazards, DHHS (NIOSH) Publication No. 2000-130. CD-Rom, July 2000.

5　Bureau of Labor Statistics. Employment Projections, Table 3b. "The 10 fastest growing occupations, 1998-2008." USDOL 99-339, November 30, 1999.

http://www.bls.gov/news.release/ecopro.t06.htm

6   Pharmacy Technician Certification Board. Pharmacy Technician Job Description, Community. http://www.ptcb.org.

7   Jeffress, Charles. OSHA Congressional Testimony: OSHA's proposed ergonomics program and its possible impact on Medicaid, Medicare, and other health care costs. 07/13/2000, presented to The Subcommittee on Employment, Safety and Training of the Senate Health, Education, Labor and Pensions Committee. http://www.osha-slc.gov/OshDoc/Testimony_data/T20000713.html

8   Borwegen, Bill. Testimony of the Service Employees International Union, AFL-CIO, CLC Before the Subcommittee on Workforce Protections Committee on Education and the Workforce. US House of Representatives. March 23, 1999.

9   Bureau of Labor Statistics. Employment Projections, Table 3b. "The 10 fastest growing occupations, 1998-2008." USDOL 99-339, November 30, 1999. http://www.bls.gov/news.release/ecopro.t06.htm

10 Department of Labor, OSHA. OSHA Summary Sheet: Workplace Violence, 1999. http://www.osha.gov/oshinfo/priorities/violence.html (reference to Warchol, Greg. Workplace Violence, 1992-96. National Crime Victimization Survey, Report No. NCJ-168634. Also, NIOSH Fact Sheet, Violence in the Workplace, 1997.)

11 Zweig, Michael. The Working Class Majority: America's Best Kept Secret. Ithaca: Cornell UP, 2000. pg. 34 - 35.

12 Zweig, Michael. The Working Class Majority: America's Best Kept Secret. Ithaca: Cornell UP, 2000. pg 4.

13 Zweig, Michael. The Working Class Majority: America's Best Kept Secret. Ithaca: Cornell UP, 2000. pg 5.

14 Zweig, Michael. The Working Class Majority: America's Best Kept Secret. Ithaca: Cornell UP, 2000. pg. 42.

Chapter 4

1   NIOSH Strategic Plan 1997 - 2002. DHHS (NIOSH) Publication No. 98-137. http://www.cdc.gov/niosh/gpran1a.html

2   DHHS, NIOSH. "Worker Health Chartbook, 2000". NIOSH Pub. No. 2000-127. page viii.

3   DHHS, NIOSH. "Worker Health Chartbook, 2000". NIOSH Pub. No. 2000-127. page 5.

4   DHHS, NIOSH. "Worker Health Chartbook, 2000". NIOSH Pub. No. 2000-127. page 14.

5   DHHS, NIOSH. "Worker Health Chartbook, 2000". NIOSH Pub. No. 2000-127. page 17.

6   Statement of Michael P. Jackson, Deputy Secretary of Transportation before the U.S. House of Representatives, June 19, 2001.

7   Statement of Michael P. Jackson, Deputy Secretary of Transportation before the U.S. House of Representatives, June 19, 2001.

8   United States. Public Law 91-596, Occupational Safety and Health Act of 1970. 91st Congress, December 29, 1970 as amended by Public Law 101-552, November 5, 1990. Section(8)(2).

9   United States. Public Law 91-596, Occupational Safety and Health Act of 1970. 91st Congress, December 29, 1970 as amended by Public Law 101-552, November 5, 1990. Section(24)(a).

10 29 CFR 1904.16.

11 Support Statement for Recording and Reporting Occupational Injuries and Illnesses,

(29 CFR 1904), Federal Register [07/07/2000] #64:42034-42035.

12   OSHA News Releases. "Ohio Auto Parts Manufacturer Settles Safety and Health Citations, Tomasco Mulciber Agrees with OSHA to Pay $820,000 in fines and Institute Comprehensive Safety and Health Program." September21, 1999. and "OSHA Proposes Fines of 1.6 Million Against Tomasco Mulciber, Inc." January 19, 1999.

13   Federal Register #62:6434-6442, 02/11/97. "Reporting Occupational Injury and Illness Data to OSHA; Final Rule. Comment made by Diantha M. Goo.

14   NIOSH does take a periodic sample of some hospital emergency departments, called the National Electronic Injury Surveillance System (NEISS). This sampling is ineffective in capturing many work-related illnesses, and overall, in capturing injuries and illnesses treated by company doctors, private doctors, and occupational health clinics.

15   Clark, Cindy and Jim Barnhardt. Phone conversations, December 15, 2000.

16   U.S. Congress, Office of Technology Assessment. "Preventing Illness and Injury in the Workplace." Washington, DC; April 1985. pg. 3.

17   Drudi, Dino. "A Century Long Quest for Meaningful and Accurate Occupational Injury and Illness Statistics." Bureau of Labor Statistics. Compensation and Working Conditions. Winter, 1997. http://www.bls.gov/osh/oshwc/osar0002.txt. The 1987 study was conducted by the National Academy of Sciences.

18   Bureau of Labor Statistics. Handbook of Methods. April, 1997. Census Definitions, pg 76.

19   BLS, Workplace Injury and Illness Summary. USDL 00-357. Press Release, December 12, 2000. http://www.bls.gov/news.release/osh.nr0.htm

20   BLS, Workplace Injury and Illness Summary. USDL 00-357. Press Release, December 12, 2000. http://www.bls.gov/news.release/osh.nr0.htm

21   OSHA Statement, "Statement of Secretary of Labor Alexis Herman on 1999 Workplace Injury and Illness Rates." December 12, 2000.

22   Wall Street Journal. August 18, 2000. pg 1.

23   The Augusta Chronicle, December 17, 1998. http://augustachronicle.com/stories/121898/bus_124-1870.shtml

24   Jeffress, Charles. Speech: "Safety and Health Challenges in the 21st Century." Presented to the American Industrial Hygiene Conference and Exposition. May, 23, 2000.

25   Cullen, Lisa. "Safety by the (Wrong) Numbers?" Occupational Hazards. October, 2000. Pg. 145-146.

26   Leigh, J. Paul, et al. "Occupational Injury and Illness in the United States." Archives of Internal Medicine. July 28, 1997;157:1557-1568.

27   Leigh, et al. Costs of Occupational Injuries and Illnesses. University of Michigan Press: Ann Arbor, 2000. pg. 6

28   Cullen, Lisa. "Safety by the (Wrong) Numbers?" Occupational Hazards. October, 2000. pg. 146. Phone interview with William Weber, BLS Assistant Commissioner for Safety, Health and Working Conditions.

29   NIOSH promises in its Chartbook, "Working with government and non-government partners, NIOSH will continue efforts to enhance occupational health surveillance in the coming years." Realistically, NIOSH alone can never fix the occupational health surveillance problem. First, national surveillance is not their mandate, it's a shared responsibility between OSHA and BLS. Second, NIOSH is inadequately funded. According to the Leigh book (pg. 259, footnote #2) NIOSH receives one of the lowest levels of funding within the Centers for Disease Control. NIOSH research awards are about one-half of one percent of the National Cancer Institute, less than one percent

of the National Institute on Aging and seven percent of the National Institute on Dental Research.

30 The Pew Environmental Health Commission Press Release, Sept. 6, 2000. "Protect Public From Chronic Diseases."

31 The Pew Environmental Health Commission. America's Environmental Health Gap: Why the Country Needs a Nationwide Health Tracking Network. Companion Report. September, 2000. pg. 4.

32 The Pew Environmental Health Commission. America's Environmental Health Gap: Why the Country Needs a Nationwide Health Tracking Network. Companion Report. September, 2000. pg. 4-5.

33 The Pew Environmental Health Commission. America's Environmental Health Gap: Why the Country Needs a Nationwide Health Tracking Network. pg. 5.

34 The Pew Environmental Health Commission. America's Environmental Health Gap: Why the Country Needs a Nationwide Health Tracking Network. September, 2000. pg. 19.

35 U.S. General Accounting Office. Toxic Chemicals: Long-Term Coordinated Strategy Needed to Measure Exposures in Humans. GAO/HEHS-00-80. May 2000. pg. 39.

36 Missoulian.com archives. Associated Press, April 28, 2000. Grace documents will be quarantined. http://www.missoulian.com/archives.

37 Missoulian.com archives. Associated Press, October 26, 2000. Disease related to asbestos could reach 15 percent. http://www.missoulian.com/archives.

38 Missoulian.com archives. Associated Press, October 26, 2000. Disease rate related to asbestos could reach 15 percent. http://www.missoulian.com/archives.

39 Missoulian.com archives. Associated Press, April 1, 2000. Asbestos found in garden products, EPA says. http://www.missoulian.com/archives.

40 29 CFR 1910.1001(c)(1) and 29 CFR 1926.1101(c)(1)

41 30 CFR 71.702 (a)

42 Schneider, Andrew. "Mine-safety agency takes action: Chief knows dangers firsthand, orders asbestos inspections." Seattle Post-Intelligencer. March 17, 2000. http://seattlep-i.nwsource.com/uncivilaction/msha17.shtml

Chapter 5

1 Glanze, Walter, et al. The Mosby Medical Encyclopedia, Plume: New York, 1985.

2 Doul, John, et al. Casarett and Doull's Toxicology. New York: Macmillan, 1980. pg 12.

3 Doul, John, et al. Casarett and Doull's Toxicology. New York: Macmillan, 1980. pg 6.

4 PELs are exposure limits based on an 8-hour workday and a 5-day work week. They must be adjusted according to length of exposure time (for example, a PEL is lowered proportionally for workers on 12-hour shifts.) In addition, OSHA allows some exposures to exceed the PEL temporarily (called short term exposure limits or ceiling concentrations) provided that the PEL average still remains below the established limit. Generally speaking, however, the PEL is most often the upper limit of allowable exposures.

5 Chemical Safety and Hazard Investigation Board. Chemsafety Fact. website http://www.csb.gov.

6 Preamble to OSHA's Methylene Chloride Standard, Section 8: Summary of the Final Economic Analysis. 62 FR 1494, January 10, 1997. http://www.osha-slc.gov/SLTC/methylenechloride/index.html.

7 Preamble to OSHA's Methylene Chloride Standard, Section 8: Summary of the Final Economic Analysis. 62 FR 1494, January 10, 1997. http://www.osha-slc.gov/SLTC/methylenechloride/index.html.

8   McDonald's Restaurant Financial Reports, 1997 Investor Factsheet. http://www.mcdonalds.com/corporate/investor/reports/factsheet/index.html

9   Preamble to OSHA's Methylene Chloride Standard, Section 3: Events Leading to the Final Standard. 62 FR 1494, January 10, 1997. http://www.osha-slc.gov/Preamble/methylch_data/METHYLENE_CL3.html

10   Preamble to OSHA's Methylene Chloride Standard, Section 3: Events Leading to the Final Standard. 62 FR 1494, January 10, 1997. http://www.osha-slc.gov/Preamble/methylch_data/METHYLENE_CL3.html

11   National Institute for Occupational Safety and Health (NIOSH), Centers for Disease Control. Criteria for a Recommended Standard: Occupational Exposure to Methylene Chloride. (75 ppm recommended only in the absence of Carbon Monoxide.) DHHS (NIOSH) Publication No. 76-138. March 1976. pg 13.

12   Preamble to OSHA's Methylene Chloride Standard, Section 3: Events Leading to the Final Standard. 62 FR 1494, January 10, 1997. http://www.osha-slc.gov/Preamble/methylch_data/METHYLENE_CL3.html

13   Preamble to OSHA's Methylene Chloride Standard, Section 3: Events Leading to the Final Standard. 62 FR 1494, January 10, 1997. http://www.osha-slc.gov/Preamble/methylch_data/METHYLENE_CL3.html

14   Preamble to OSHA's Methylene Chloride Standard, Section 3: Events Leading to the Final Standard. 62 FR 1494, January 10, 1997. http://www.osha-slc.gov/Preamble/methylch_data/METHYLENE_CL3.html

15   Preamble to OSHA's Methylene Chloride Standard, Section 3: Events Leading to the Final Standard. 62 FR 1494, January 10, 1997. http://www.osha-slc.gov/Preamble/methylch_data/METHYLENE_CL3.html

16   National Institute for Occupational Safety and Health (NIOSH), Centers for Disease Control. Current Intelligence Bulletin 46, Methylene Chloride. April 18, 1986. http://www.cdc.gov/niosh/86114_46.html.

17   National Institute for Occupational Safety and Health (NIOSH), Centers for Disease Control, Current Intelligence Bulletin Number 46. April 18, 1986.

18   OSHA. Advance Notice of Proposed Rulemaking [51 FR 42257]. November 24, 1986.

19   Preamble to OSHA's Methylene Chloride Standard, Section 8: Summary of the Final Economic Analysis. 62 FR 1494, January 10, 1997. http://www.osha-slc.gov/SLTC/methylenechloride/index.html.

20   Halogenated Solvents Industry Alliance, Inc. White Paper on Methylene Chloride June 1998. http://www.hsia.org/methchlor.htm (the U.S. demand for MC in 1996, the year before OSHA reduced the MC PEL, was 285 million pounds.)

21   Preamble to OSHA's Methylene Chloride Standard, Section 8: Summary of the Final Economic Analysis. 62 FR 1494, January 10, 1997. http://www.osha-slc.gov/SLTC/methylenechloride/index.html.

22 Preamble to OSHA's Methylene Chloride Standard, Section 5: Health Effects. 62 FR 1494, January 10, 1997. http://www.osha-slc.gov/SLTC/methylenechloride/index.html.

23   In its April, 2000 Semi-Annual Regulatory Agenda, for example, OSHA summarized the ongoing situation: "OSHA enforces hundreds of permissible exposure limits (PELs) for toxic air contaminants found in U.S. workplaces. OSHA adopted most of the air contaminant limits in 1971 from recommendations issued by the American Conference of Governmental Industrial Hygienists and the American National Standards Institute. These PELs, which have not been updated since 1971, thus reflect the results of research conducted in the 1950s and 1960s. Since then, much new information has become available that indicates that, in many cases, these early limits are outdated and insufficiently protective of worker health. To correct this situation, OSHA issued a

final rule in 1989; it lowered the existing PELs for 212 toxic air contaminants and established PELs for 164 previously unregulated air contaminants. On June 12, 1992, OSHA proposed a rule that would have extended these limits to workplaces in the construction, maritime, and agriculture industries. However, on July 10, 1992, the Eleventh Circuit Court of Appeals vacated the 1989 final rule on the grounds that "(1) OSHA failed to establish that existing exposure limits in the workplace presented significant risk of material health impairment or that new standards eliminated or substantially lessened the risk; (2) OSHA did not meet its burden of establishing that its 428 new permissible exposure limits (PELs) were either economically or technologically feasible." The Court's decision forced the Agency to return to the earlier, insufficiently protective limits."

24 OSHA. Brief for the Secretary of Labor; AFL-CIO v. OSHA/USDOL, In the United States Court of Appeals for the Eleventh Circuit, On Petition for Review of a Final Rule of the Occupational Safety and Health Administration; SOL No. 24008905567; 1990. http://www.osha.gov/oshinfo/priorities/pel.html.

25 de la Cruz, Peter L. and David Sarvadi. "OSHA PELs: Where Do We Go From Here?" American Industrial Hygiene Journal. 55.10. October 1994. pg. 896.

26 The OSHA Act. Section (6)(b)(5).

27 Proposed Information Collection Request, Federal Register 61:48983-48985 09/17/1996

28 OSHA's Methylene Chloride Standard Preamble.

29 Preamble to OSHA's Methylene Chloride Standard, Section 6: Quantitative Risk Analysis. 62 FR 1494, January 10, 1997. http://www.osha-slc.gov/SLTC/methylenechloride/index.html.

30 NIOSH. Criteria Document, Revised Recommendation for an Occupational Exposure Standard for Benzene. Cincinnati, OH. 1976.

31 Supreme Court of the United States. 448 U.S. 607, 100 S. Ct. 2844. FN9.

32 Supreme Court of the United States. 448 U.S. 607, 100 S. Ct. 2844.

33 Supreme Court of the United States. 448 U.S. 607, 100 S. Ct. 2844.

34 Nicholson, William J. and Philip J. Landrigan. "Quantitative Assessment of Lives Lost Due to Delay in the Regulation of Occupational Exposure to Benzene." Environmental Health Perspectives 82 (1989): 185-188.

35 Public Affairs Television, Inc. "Trade Secrets: A Moyers Report." Televised on the Public Broadcasting System, March 26, 2001.

36 OSHA. PEL's Update. http://www.osha.gov/oshinfo/priorities/pel.html.

37 NIOSH. NIOSH Pocket Guide to Chemical Hazards and other databases. CD-Rom. DHHS (NIOSH) Publication No. 2000-130, July 2000.

38 ACGIH. 2001 Guide to Occupational Exposure Values.

39 Mirer, Franklin. "The Future of Industrial Hygiene." American Academy of Industrial Hygiene Newsletter, Sept. 1998: 98-3. pg. 4.

40 NIOSH. Hazard Control 17, Control of Exposure to Perchloroethylene in Commercial Drycleaning (Substitution). http://www.cdc.gov/niosh/hc17.html

41 NIOSH. NIOSH Pocket Guide to Chemical Hazards and other databases. CD-Rom. DHHS (NIOSH) Publication No. 2000-130, July 2000.

42 Halogenated Solvents Industry Alliance. Halogenated Solvents Industry Alliance Update, Nov./Dec. 1999. pg 2. http://www.hsia.org/updates/update-list.htm

43 OSHA comments from the June 19, 1988 Final Rule on Air Contaminants Project extracted from 54FR2324 et. seq. (This rule was remanded by the U.S. Circuit Court of Appeals and the limits are not currently in force.) http://www.cdc.gov/niosh/pel88/127-18.html

44 OSHA Unified Agenda, Proposed Rule Stage. 2247, Occupational Exposure to

Hexavalent Chromium (Preventing Occupational Illness: Chromium) Nov. 30, 2000. http://www.osha-slc.gov/Reg_Agenda_data/2247.html

45 Vladeck, David C. Testimony before the Senate Committee on Governmental Affairs on S. 746, The Regulatory Improvement Act of 1999. April 21, 1999.

46 OSHA's Office of Public Affairs, E-mail correspondence, March 29, 2001. ETSs for vinyl chloride, dibromo-3-chloropropane and the first ETS on asbestos were not challenged. They continued in effect for the entire six month period until superseded by final standards. An ETS on acrylonitrile was challenged; however, the requested stay was denied by the Sixth Circuit Court of Appeals. Four ETSs (benzene, commercial diving, pesticides, and 14 carcinogens) were stayed or vacated by courts of appeal. A second asbestos ETS was stayed by the Fifth Circuit Court of Appeals in March 1984.

Chapter 6

1   Pepper, Timothy G. "Understanding OSHA: A Look at the Agency's Complex Legal & Political Environment." Professional Safety. pg 15.

2   Umbrell, Christine. "Stepping Up to the Plate." The Synergist, December, 2000. pg. 26.

3   Umbrell, Christine. "Stepping Up to the Plate." The Synergist, December, 2000. pg. 27.

4   Lewis, Charles. The Buying of the Congress: How Special Interests Have Stolen your Right to Life, Liberty and the Pursuit of Happiness. New York: Avon, 1998. pg 170.

5   Nash, Jim. "Can OSHA Bridge the Ergonomics Gap?" Occupational Hazards. May 2000. pg. 16.

6   National Coalition on Ergonomics, website. http://www.ncergo.org/suits.htm. 1/7/01.

7   OSHA,OSHA Summary Sheet: PELs Update. http://www.osha.gov/oshinfo/priorities/pel.html.

8   Volante, Enric and Rhonda Bodfield Sander. "Protection didn't work so 25 workers poisoned by beryllium now risk death." Arizona Daily Star. May 9, 1999.

9   Volante, Enric and Rhonda Bodfield Sander. "Protection didn't work so 25 workers poisoned by beryllium now risk death." Arizona Daily Star. May 9, 1999.

10 Volante, Enric and Rhonda Bodfield Sander. "Protection for workers stymied by firm, allies." Arizona Daily Star. May 9, 1999.

11 Volante, Enric and Rhonda Bodfield Sander. "Protection didn't work so 25 workers poisoned by beryllium now risk death." Arizona Daily Star. May 9, 1999.

12 Volante, Enric and Rhonda Bodfield Sander. "Protection didn't work so 25 workers poisoned by beryllium now risk death." Arizona Daily Star. May 9, 1999.

13 Steingraber, Sandra. Living Downstream. New York: Vintage Books, 1997. pg. 73

14 Baier, Edward J. Statement to Department of Labor, OSHA, Public Hearing on the Occupational Standard for Beryllium. August 19, 1977.

15 Jameson, C. W. Introduction to the Conference on Beryllium-related Diseases. Environ Health Perspect 104(Suppl 5):935-936 (1996).

16 OSHA Unified Agenda, Long Term Actions. Occupational Exposure to Beryllium. Nov. 22, 1999. http://www.osha-slc.gov/Reg_Agenda_data/2172.html.

17 Collins, Martha. "OSHA's Safety and Health Program Standard." The Synergist. April, 1998. pg. 24.

18 U.S. Chamber of Commerce. Press Release, March 23, 1999. http://uschamber.com/media/releases/March99/032399.htm.

19 Prepared testimony of Mr. Lawrence P. Halprin, Partner, Keller & Heckman, LLP. http://www.house.gov/smbiz/hearings/106th/1999/0990722/halprin.htm

20 Lewis, Charles. The Buying of the Congress: How Special Interests Have Stolen your Right to Life, Liberty and the Pursuit of Happiness. New York: Avon, 1998. pg. 170-171.

21 Department of Labor, OSHA. "OSHA policies concerning employees working at home." OSHA Standard Interpretation and Compliance Letter, Response # 2. Nov. 15, 1999. Withdrawn, Jan 5, 2000.

22 Department of Labor, OSHA. "OSHA policies concerning employees working at home." OSHA Standard Interpretation and Compliance Letter, Response # 3. Nov. 15, 1999. Withdrawn, Jan 5, 2000.

23 Swoboda, Frank and Kirstin Downey Grimsley. "OSHA covers at-home workers; Companies liable for safety of telecommuters." Washington Post, January 4, 2000. pg A01.

24 "Inside Washington." The Synergist. May 2000, pg. 10.

25 "OSHA Stumbles on Information Age." Occupational Hazards. March, 2000. pg. 8

26 Thornton, James. "Letter to John Stossel, ABC News 20/20." The Synergist. March 2000, pg 9.

27 Hironaka, Jolani and Amy Dean. Letter to the Editor, "OSHA's Turnaround." Washington Post. January 18, 2000.

28 Bureau of Labor Statistics. "Work at Home in 1977." March 11, 1998 News Release. USDL-98-93. http://stats.bls.gov/newsrels.htm.

29 OSHA Act. Section 2. Public Law 91-596, As amended by Public Law 101-552.

30 Department of Labor, OSHA. OSHA Instruction, Directive Number CPL2-0.125. Home-Based Worksites. February 25, 2000.

31 Umbrell, Christine. "Stepping Up to the Plate." The Synergist. December, 2000. pg. 28.

32 OSHA's website, Frequently Asked Questions. http://www.osha-slc.gov/html/faq-various.html

33 Eric Schlosser, "Fast Food Nation: The Dark Side of the All-American Meal." Houghton Mifflin Company, Boston. pg. 84-85.

34 Fax transmittal from Bill Wright, OSHA Office of Public Affairs. April 2, 2001.

35 National Fire Protection Association website. An Overview of NFPA. http://www.nfpa.org/About_NFPA/An_Overview_of_NFPA/an_overview_of_nfpa.html

36 National Fire Protection Association. Life Safety Code, NFPA 101:13-2.3.4. 1994 Edition. pg. 101-131/

37 American National Standards Association website. National Standardization. http://web.ansi.org/public/ansi_info/national.html

38 The Synergist. ANSI Updates. December, 2000. pg. 35.

39 Email correspondence from Bill Wright. OSHA Office of Public Affairs. March 29, 2001.

40 U.S. Office of Management and Budget. October 20, 1993. Circular A-119.

41 OMB Circular A-119; Federal Participation in the Development and Use of Voluntary Consensus Standards and in Conformity Assessment Activities; [Federal Register: February 19, 1998 (Volume 63, Number 33)] pg. 8545-8558.
http://ts.nist.gov/ts/htdocs/210/215/omb/taba.htm

42 Refractory Ceramic Fibers Coalition. "ACGIH Update." March 15, 2001.

43 Refractory Ceramic Fibers Coalition website. http://www.rcfc.net/about.htm

44 ACGIH. 2001 TLVs and BEIs. pg 54.

45 2001 TLVs and BEIs. ACGIH, 2001. The full ACGIH policy statement on the uses of TLV's and BEI's is much more extensive and can be found in the front inside cover of each TLV/BEI booklet.

46   ACGIH Press Release. ACGIH/RCFC Lawsuit Settled. July 2, 2001.

47   ACGIH website. http://www.acgih.org/members/CaseStudies.htm

48   Wyoming Mining Association website. http://www.wma-minelife.com/trona/TronaPage/tronainf.htm

49   ACGIH 2001 TLVs and BEIs. Notice of Intended Changes for 2001. Page 64.

50   Solvay Minerals, Inc. Material Safety Data Sheet #008. Revised May 11, 2000. Product: natural sodium sesquicarbonate. pg. 2.

51   ACGIH Trona Settlement Public Statement, posted September 13, 2001 at www.acgih.org

Chapter 7

1   OSHA. Ergonomics: The Study of Work. Publication 3125, revised 2000. pg. 4.

2   U.S. Congress, Office of Technology Assessment. Preventing Illness and Injury in the Workplace. OTA-H-256. Washington, DC: April, 1985. pg. 3.

3   Centers for Disease Control, NIOSH, Musculoskeletal Disorders and Workplace Factors. July, 1997. http://www.cdc.gov/niosh/ergosci1.html?#executivesum?

4   United States Senate. Subcommittee on Public Health and Safety of the Committee on Labor and Human Resources. Hearing on Oversight of OSHA/OSHA Reinvention. Prepared Statement of Mike Lail on behalf of The Associated General Contractors of America. 105th Cong. 1st Sess. Washington: GPO, July 10, 1997. pg. 82.

5   United States House of Representatives. Committee on Small Business. Hearing on Bill HR 3234, "Small Business OSHA Relief Act." Testimony of Ed Hayden, Safety and Health Director, The Associated General Contractors of America-Milwaukee Chapter. 104th Cong., 2nd Sess. Washington: GPO, September 25, 1996. pg 65.

6   The National Association of Manufacturers. Press Release—Ergonomics. "NAM Praises Passage of Ergonomics Bill in House." August 4, 1999.

7   Sarvadi, David. Keller and Heckman, llp. Presentation to the Lehigh Valley Section of the American Industrial Hygiene Association. April 12, 2000.

8   NCE website. Fact Sheet. http://www.ncergo.org/facts.htm#factsheet.

9   The Food Marketing Institute website. product available: "Suggestions for Ergonomic Improvement of Scanning Checkstand Designs, 1992. http://www.fmi.org/pub/Pubs_searchresults.cfm?prod_id=683.

10   The Food Marketing Institute website. product available: "Ergonomics & Order Selecting: A Guide for Distribution Center Supervisors." video, 1995http:www.fmi.org/pub/Pubs_searchresults.cfm?prod-id=811.

11   The Food Marketing Institute website. product available: "Final Report of FMI's Ergonomics Task Force, 1996." http:www.fmi.org/pub/Pubs_searchresults.cfm?prod-id=953

12   Charles Jeffress, speech to The National Coalition on Ergonomics, April 29, 1999.

13   United States Government Accounting Office. Report to Congressional Requesters. "Worker Protection - Private Sector Ergonomics Programs Yield Positive Results." GAO/HEHS-97-163, Washington, DC. Letter to The Honorable Edward M. Kennedy, Ranking Minority Member, Committee on Labor and Human Resources, United States Senate and The Honorable Major Owens, Ranking Minority Member, Subcommittee on Workforce Protections, Committee on Education and the Workforce, House of Representatives. August 27, 1997. http://www.cdc.gov/niosh/gaoergo.html

14   United States Government Accounting Office. Report to Congressional Requesters. "Worker Protection - Private Sector Ergonomics Programs Yield Positive Results." GAO/HEHS-97-163, Washington, DC. Letter to The Honorable Edward M. Kennedy,

Ranking Minority Member, Committee on Labor and Human Resources, United States Senate and The Honorable Major Owens, Ranking Minority Member, Subcommittee on Workforce Protections, Committee on Education and the Workforce, House of Representatives. August 27, 1997. http://www.cdc.gov/niosh/gaoergo.html

15   Charles Jeffress, speech to The National Coalition on Ergonomics, April 29, 1999

16   Statement from Ed Gilroy, co-chair of the National Coalition on Ergonomics responding to the pending release of OSHA's ergonomics rule. 11/21/99

17   Doyle, Jack. Taken for a Ride: Detroit's Big Three and the Politics of Pollution. New York: Four Walls Eight Windows, 2000. pg. 8.

18   Waldman, Peter. "Dangerous Waters. All Agree that Arsenic Kills; The Question Is How Much It Takes to Do So." The Wall Street Journal. April 19, 2001. page 1.

19   Waldman, Peter. "Dangerous Waters. All Agree that Arsenic Kills; The Question Is How Much It Takes to Do So." The Wall Street Journal. April 19, 2001. page 1.

20   Waldman, Peter. "Dangerous Waters. All Agree that Arsenic Kills; The Question Is How Much It Takes to Do So." The Wall Street Journal. April 19, 2001. page 1.

21   OSHA's Website, Ergonomics Page. http://www.osha-slc.gov/SLTC/ergonomics/index.html

22   United States Government Accounting Office. Report to Congressional Requesters. "Worker Protection - Private Sector Ergonomics Programs Yield Positive Results." GAO/HEHS-97-163, Washington, DC. Letter to The Honorable Edward M. Kennedy, Ranking Minority Member, Committee on Labor and Human Resources, United States Senate and The Honorable Major Owens, Ranking Minority Member, Subcommittee on Workforce Protections, Committee on Education and the Workforce, House of Representatives. August 27, 1997. http://www.cdc.gov/niosh/gaoergo.html

23   Occupational Safety and Health Act, Occupational Safety and Health Standards Section, Section Number 6 (b)(5). online at http://www.osha-slc.gov/OshAct_data/OSH_ACT6.html

24   United States House of Representatives. Committee on Small Business. Hearing on Bill HR 3234, "Small Business OSHA Relief Act." Testimony of Ed Hayden, Safety and Health Director, The Associated General Contractors of America-Milwaukee Chapter. 104th Cong., 2nd Sess. Washington: GPO, September 25, 1996. pgs 12 - 13.

25   Humantech, Inc. Applied Ergonomics Manual. self-published, 1989, revised 1995. page 113.

26   Humantech, Inc. Applied Ergonomics Manual. self-published, 1989, revised 1995. page 117.

27   "Ergonomic Solutions for a New Millenium. "Lehigh Valley Section of the American Industrial Hygene Association: Bethlehem, PA. April , 2000.

28   Guetschow, Joan. "Attorney Shares Insight on Legal Challenges Against OSHA." Ergonomics Today. December 11, 2000. http://www.ergoweb.com/news/detail.cfm?id=224

29   Statement by the President. March 21, 2001. The White House, Office of the Press Secretary.

30   For the Record. "From remarks by House Minority Leader Dick Gephardt (D-Mo)during a news conference yesterday at the Capital. The Washington Post, March 8, 2001.

31   "Congress Kills Ergo Rule—Now What?" Occupational Hazards Magazine. April, 2001. pg. 14.

Chapter 8

1   Section one of the OSHA Act. Public Law 91-596, as amended by Public Law 101-552, section 3101, November 5, 1990.

2   OSHA's Field Inspection Reference Manual. Section 5, Chapter I (c)(4)(a). It reads, "...All pertinent information will be entered on an OSHA-7 form, or equivalent, by the complainant or a member of the Area OSHA staff. A copy of this completed form can be sent to the complainant for signature, or the complainant shall be asked to sign a letter with the particular details of the complaint to the area office."

3   OSHA's Field Inspection Reference Manual. Section 5, Chapter 1 (E)(3).

4   29 CFR 1910.1052(f)(3)(i)

5   OSHA DATA Report, from OSHA's IMIS database. August 23, 2000.

6   OSHA DATA Report, from OSHA's IMIS database. Average Unclassifieds issued from 1989 to 1999.

7   Crouse-Hinds, Division of Cooper Industries case file for inspection # 106901085. Wolf Street and 7th North Street, Syracuse, NY. OSHA 1-B worksheet form.

8   Cooper Industries website. http://www.cooperindustries.com/index.htm.

9   OSHA Worksheet. OSHA-1B. August 12, 1999. Number 20.

10   OSHA Worksheet. OSHA-1B. August 12, 1999. Number 20(a).

11   per the OSHA Worksheet August 12, 1999, Gravity Based Penalties set at $70,000.

12   The citation was for OSHA's Electrical, Wiring Methods, Components & Equipment standard.

13   The actual language read, "This Settlement Agreement covers violations of the Occupational Safety and Health Act ("the Act") that are alleged in connection with the Inspection, and any and all citation items and notifications of penalty that are to be issued in connection with the Inspection."

14   AFL-CIO. Death on the Job: The Toll of Neglect. 9th Edition. April 2000. pg. 3.

15   OSHA Fact Sheet 92-36. New OSHA Civil Penalties Policy. 01/01/92. pg. 1.

16   OSHA Data. Verbal report of average OSHA penalty reductions by type, May 3, 2001.

17   U.S. Dept. of Labor, OSHA. All About OSHA. Publication 2056, revised 2000. pg. 31-32—answers the question "What Happens After an OSHA Inspection?" by saying "Under the OSHA Act, OSHA may cite the following violations and propose the following penalties..." and it goes on to list only the traditional other-than-serious, serious, willful, repeat, and failure-to-abate.

18   OSHA 3000 booklet. Employer Rights and Responsibilities Following an OSHA Inspection. 1999. Page three specifically responds to the commonly asked question, "What are the types of violations?" by listing only the traditional willful, serious, repeat and other. The unclassified is not mentioned anywhere in the violation explanation or, in fact, anywhere in the 34 page pamphlet,

19   OSHA's Field Inspection Reference Manual. Section 8, Chapter four (D)(4)(a)(2)(a)

20   OSHA's Field Inspection Reference Manual. Section 8, Chapter four (D)(4)(a)(2)(b)

21   OSHA DATA report. May 3, 2001. Unclassified initial penalty for FY 10/01/99 to 09/30/2000 was $12,198 and final penalty was $8,926.

22   OSHA is calling the initial violations "post settlement," yet another made-up violation type, and then later changing them to unclassified to hide the real original violation. In reality, OSHA is issuing unclassifieds initially and just calling them post settlement. Then, in the Settlement Agreement, they are changed to unclassifieds.

23   OSHA's Field Inspection Reference Manual. Section 8, Chapter four (D)(4)(a)(2)(a).

24   From January 1, 1999 to June 30, 2000, unclassifieds were issued in a total of 165 cases. Of those 165 cases, 116 cases (70%) were closed, meaning they were completely settled. The 116 closed cases received 259 unclassifieds, broken down in the following way: 136 received initial type U violation and closed with 136 type U; 55 received initial type S violation and closed with 51 type U violation; 51 received initial type W violation and closed with 51 type U violation; 16 received initial type R violation and

closed with 16 type U violation; 1 received initial type O violation and closed with 1 type U violation. Source OSHA Data report from OSHA's IMIS database.

25 OSHA Standards Interpretation and Compliance Letters. 8/14/91. Memo to All Regional Administrators, from Patricia K. Clark, Directorate of Compliance Programs, through Leo Carey, Office of Field Programs. Subject: Section 17 Designation.

26 OSHA Standards Interpretation and Compliance Letters. 8/14/91. Memo to All Regional Administrators, from Patricia K. Clark, Directorate of Compliance Programs, through Leo Carey, Office of Field Programs. Subject: Section 17 Designation.

27 Mulder, James. T. "Crouse-Hinds agrees to pay $350,000 fine." Post-Standard, Syracuse Newspapers. July 27, 1999. pg. A-1.

28 Bureau of National Affairs, Occupational Safety & Health Reporter. (Vol. 27, No. 8, page 244.) Special Report: Enforcement, OSHA Settlement Agreements. 7/3/97.

29 Bureau of National Affairs, Occupational Safety & Health Reporter. (Vol. 27, No. 8, page 244.) Special Report: Enforcement, OSHA Settlement Agreements. 7/3/97.

30 McCalla, Thompson website. http://www.mtphs.com/Practice/repwork/repsafe.htm

31 OSHA's Field Inspection Reference Manual. Section 8, Chapter four (D)(4)(a)(2)

32 OSHA's Field Inspection Reference Manual. Section 8, Chapter four (C)(2)(i)(5)(a)

33 OSHA DATA report, from OSHA's IMIS database. August 23, 2000.

34 The settlement agreement read, "The penalty for Citation No. 1, Item 1 is reduced from $7,000 to $5,000. The penalty for Citation No. 1, Item 2 is reduced from $2,000 to $1,000. Items 1a and 1d of Citation No. 2 are amended to Items 1a and 1b of Serious Citation No. 4 and a penalty of $3,000 is assessed for this Item. Citation No. 2, Items 1b and 1c are amended by deleting the "willful" classification of the violation and reclassifying this item as a violation of "Section 17 of the Act." The penalty for Citation No. 2, Items 1b and 1c is reduced from $70,000 to $47,000."

35 August 23, 1996 letter to Senators Paul Simon and Ed Kennedy. Occupational Safety and Health: Violations of Safety and Health Regulations by Federal Contractors, August 1996. GAO/HEHS-96-157.

36 Occupational Safety and Health: Violations of Safety and Health Regulations by Federal Contractors. Background. August 1996. GAO/HEHS-96-157.

Chapter 9

1 The Center for Public Integrity. Citizen Muckraking: How to Investigate and Right Wrongs in Your Community. Common Courage Media: Monroe, ME. pg. 17.

2 State-run OSHAs were excluded since they rarely issue unclassifieds. The 25 sample cases were selected from a list of unclassified recipients that also had received deletions. Employers were construction and general industry businesses that had had fatalities, explosions or just got caught breaking OSHA law. Four cases were settled by the OSHA Review Commission, the rest by informal settlement agreements. All requested files were for closed cases from 1999 and 2000, therefore, they were disclosable under FOIA. The FOIA request asked for copies of all OSHA documentation pertaining to the inspection and settlement, including: complaint or accident report, inter-office or inter-agency memos, phone logs, summary reports, field notes and logs, settlement agreements, solicitor's notes, sampling and analysis data, and all other pertinent investigation or settlement information.

3 Most commonly, these files consisted of: The Citation and Notification of Penalty; Informal Settlement Agreement; and Inspection Report.

4 OSHA Instruction CPL-2.45B, CH-4, December 13, 1993. Office of General Industry Compliance Assistance. (A)(1)(a) and (b).

5 OSHA Instruction CPL-2.45B, CH-4, December 13, 1993. Office of General Industry

Compliance Assistance. (b)(4)(a).

6   Items blacked-out included: penalty reduction factors (standard adjustments made in consideration of employer size, good faith and history); factors to determine the gravity-based-penalty (severity of hazard, probability of risk, and gravity of potential/actual injury); and the classification of the violation (whether it was serious, willful or repeated and whether the employer had knowledge of it.) Inexplicably, the deletions were noted as allowable under FOIA exemption 5, which says: "Inter-agency or intra-agency memorandums or letters only available by law to a party in litigation with the agency."

7   FOIA. U.S. Code: Title 5, Section 552(a)(4)(A)(II)(iii) which reads, "Documents shall be furnished without any charge or at a charge reduced below the fees established under clause (ii) if disclosure of the information is in the public interest because it is likely to contribute significantly to public understanding of the operations or activities of the government and is not primarily in the commercial interest of the requester."

8   IMIS inspection reports provided by OSHA's Office of Management Data Systems. Run 11-06-2000, National summary by region, federal data. National summary by region, state data.

9   OSHA National News Release, USDL: 00-89. March 26, 2000. http://www.osha.gov/media/oshnews/mar00/national-20000324.html.

10   OSHA has released online the total list of 13,000 employers with injury and illness rates above 8. This huge list, however, is essentially useless to anyone except persons trying to sell safety and health services. The list is online at http://www.osha-slc.gov/html/hot_5.html.

11   OSHA was simply refusing to give me the data. OSHA's refusal said, "OSHA has not sorted its DCI records by employer size group, has not classified its records by these groupings and has no programative need to do so. Agencies are not required to sort data so as to create new records." True, OSHA did not have to do this. The "sorting" would have involved adding approximately 15 new fields to the database and hitting the enter button, a task that would have taken perhaps 30 minutes at the most. The fact that the agency would not cooperate on this minimal request that would have so much return for the nation really illustrates their fear of Congress and industry lawsuits.

12   IMIS reported 63 violations, for example, for Crouse Hinds Division of Cooper Industries in Syracuse, NY. On January 26, 1999, a 43-year old male mechanic died when the machine he was working in started unexpectedly. The IMIS table of violations is three pages long. One line reads, "ID: 01012, Type: Unclass, Standard: 19100146C02, Issuance: 07/23/99, Abate: 09/01/99, Curr$:5500, Init$: 5500, Fta$: 0.00, Contest: left blank, LastEvent: left blank.

Translated, this means that violation number 12 was issued as an unclassified violation (rather than a willful, serious, repeat or other) for a violation of the confined space regulation, section (c)(2). Issued on July 23, 1999 (six months after the fatality) and fixed (abated) on September 1, 1999 (8 months after the fatality and 6 weeks after the citation was issued), the initial penalty was for $5,500 and the final penalty was $5,500. Violation number 12 is one of 63 issued after the mechanic's death. Seven workers were exposed in six instances.

To understand what exactly what the employer did wrong to receive violation number 12, a person reading IMIS needs to know that "Standard 19100146C02" means the confined space regulation found in the 29th Code of Federal Regulations (29 CFR) section 1910.146. The actual confined space regulation can be found in another part of the OSHA website.

A person considering working for, purchasing from or investing in Crouse Hinds would probably like to know its history of safety and health violations but IMIS is not a feasible source of information. It is simply too unknown and complicated. Even the socially responsible investment community—companies with professional researchers that invest billions of dollars in businesses that take care of the public, their workers and the environment—express frustration at not being able to obtain good injury and illness data. Other than buying a company-specific report from Matt, there is no workable tool available for either the press, the public, or the investment community to evaluate a company's safety and health performance.

To start using IMIS, go to http://www.osha.gov. Scroll down and click on "Library/Reading room." Next, click on "Statistics & Inspection Data." To sort by name, use the "Establishment Search" feature. Narrow the search by making it as specific as possible by state and/or by date. After the search, scroll down to the company name and click on the left column to put a check in the box. If the company has had numerous inspections, click on numerous boxes. Each is for just one inspection (by inspection number). Go back to the top of the report and click on "get detail" to see the details for those individual company inspections.

Index

Acknowledgments

I first told my husband, then-boyfriend, about my idea for this book over eight years ago. He quipped, "You should do it." Since then, he has supported my every effort, paid each bill without question or complaint, and never once meddled in the content. There were countless nights and weekends where he sacrificed his time so I could research or write. I would not have made it along what became a long and strained journey without his steady love, encouragement and support. His computer trouble-shooting skills didn't hurt either.

I must thank my entire family for not telling me what a crazy idea it was to stop working to write a book even though I knew nothing about writing a book. Throughout all the publisher rejections (I lost count after 32), delays and re-writes, my family sweat it out with me, especially my mother. Not one negative word was uttered despite year after year of asking, "How's the book coming along?" I am grateful they kept asking and believing it was still coming along. Sometimes, I was not sure myself.

Throughout every page of this book, the voices from interviews with injured and ill workers speak. Whether quoted or not, all their experiences are reflected because each influenced the path this book took. The first three chapters were entirely different until I began interviewing workers; then, I realized I had to discuss workers compensation. I am grateful for the trust and courage it took to grant me—usually a stranger on the phone referred by another injured worker or a lawyer—such intimate insight into personal, painful experiences. Not only was I granted interviews—sometimes with two or three callbacks for more details—but I was sent medical files, inspection reports, copies of OSHA forms and even personal diaries so I could understand what happened and the effects and suffering endured. This book is infinitely better because these people chose to open their hearts, bare their scars and share their stories.

I include a special note of gratitude for Ron Hayes, founder of Families In Grief Hold Together (The FIGHT Project). Ever since I called him for an interview, Ron never wavered in his belief that this book would become a reality. He has been a friend and source of personal encouragement as well as a resource for questions about FOIA and OSHA inspection experiences. I thank him for all his help, but most of all, for the many times he said, "Don't worry, it will happen. God has a plan."

Matt Carmel at OSHA Data is a pleasure to know and was a huge help throughout much of my research. Matt always responded when asked for information and never charged me for it. One of the great things about Matt is that he is one of the few professionals I know that cares enough to be upset and even disgusted. During one of our first meetings, he warned me that no one will care about the data I was sifting through and sorting and re-sorting until it made sense (OSHA's Unclassified violations). I am grateful for Matt's freely shared information, his insights, and most of all, his outrage.

My editor, Arthur Stamoulis, took this book and made it publishable. I thank him for consistently holding the bar high and skillfully showing me how to get there. I am especially grateful for his merciless application of the word "redundant." Without Arthur, this book would read like a science dictionary written by an overly analytical and irritated bore. I also owe much to Greg Bates at Common Courage Press. From the beginning, he found the issue worthy and wanted to publish it. I am grateful for this as well as for his trust and integrity.

Lisa Koene deserves special thanks for housing me while I spent weeks researching at the Library of Congress and the National Library of Medicine. Not only did she make the research possible by eliminating unaffordable hotel bills, she made it fun and easy. Without my dear friend Lisa, I might still be lost on the Metro somewhere in DC.

I wish to thank Emily Craddock who cheerfully played with my rambunctious son for an entire summer so I could have uninterrupted phone interviews. Hers was an incredibly important role in producing this book.

Finally, I am grateful to the First United Methodist Church members who prayed with me from the beginning to put the book in God's hands. Many times, I remembered that prayer and released what otherwise would have become an unbearable burden. Ultimately, God gets all the credit for steering the resources, people, direction and timing to bring this book about.